# MODELBUILDER'S NOTEBOOK:

## A Guide for Architects, Landscape Architects, and Interior Designers

Fuller Moore

McGraw-Hill Publishing Company

New York    St. Louis    San Francisco    Auckland    Bogotá    Caracas    Hamburg    Lisbon    London
Madrid    Mexico    Milan    Montreal    New Delhi    Oklahoma City    Paris    San Juan    São Paulo
Singapore    Sidney    Tokyo    Toronto

Library of Congress Cataloging-in-Publication Data

Moore, Fuller.
     Modelbuilder's notebook: a guide for architects and
   interior designers / Fuller Moore.
              p.     cm.
Includes bibliographical references.
ISBN  0-07-043026-8
1. Architectural models.   2. Interior decoration - Models.
I. Title.    II. Title: Modelbuilder's notebook.
NA2790.M6      1990
720'.228-dc20                                        89-13840

MODELBUILDER'S  NOTEBOOK
A Guide for Architects, Landscape Architects, and Interior Designers

1 2 3 4 5 6 7 8 9 0    KGP       KGP   9 5 4 3 2 1 0
ISBN  0-07-043026-8

The type and book design was done by the author.
The editors were B. J. Clark and Jack Maisel.
The production supervisor was Richard Ausburn.
Arcata Graphics / Kingsport was printer and binder.

# TABLE OF CONTENTS

1. **INTRODUCTION**     1
The design / presentation continuum 1; The design study model 2; The presentation model 5;
Scale 6; Other model types 9

2. **TOOLS AND SUPPLIES**     10
Cutting tools 10; Drafting tools 12; Painting tools 13; Power tools 15; Supplies 16; Adhesives 21; Wood strips 22;
Coatings and rendering materials 23

3. **THE MODEL BASE**     29
Subbase 29; Enlarging the site plan 30; Base topography 33; "Slipped sheathing" contours 37;
Spaced chipboard contours 39; Finished chipboard contours 40; Acrylic model covers 43

4. **LANDSCAPE FEATURES**     45
Trees and shrubs 44; Scale figures 49; Vehicles 50; Water 52; Rock outcroppings 54

5. **SMALL-SCALE BUILDINGS**     55
Scale 55; Photocopied facades 56; Foam board 57; Carved foam 57; Wood 57; Clay 58

6. **MEDIUM-SCALE BUILDINGS**     59
Interior visibility 59; Wall thickness 60; Sheet material selection 61; Construction sequence 62;
Layout 63; Rendering surfaces 66; Cutting components 69; Color cut edges 70; Component assembly 71;
Installing the building 73; Building accessories 74; Landscape accessories 76

7. **INTERIOR MODELS**     77
Detailed room models 77; Layout 77; Rendering the floor 78; Interior partitions 79; Furniture 80;
Plants 82; Rugs and carpet 82; Draperies 82; Perimeter walls 83; Exposed roof trusses 83;
Ceiling 83; Electric lighting 84; Furniture layout models 86

8. **MODEL PHOTOGRAPHY**     88
Shoot location 90; Space and depth 91; Sky backdrops 94; Lighting 96; Viewpoint 99; Cameras 102; Film 103;
Exposure 104; Lenses 105; Depth of field 107; Perspective control 108

TABLE OF CONTENTS (continued) _____

**REFERENCES**                                                                    110

**Appendix  A:  RECIPES  FOR  RENDERING  BUILDING  MATERIALS**                     111
    Brick masonry 111; Stipple-textured surfaces 113; Cut limestone, unpainted concrete block 114;
    Field stone masonry 115; Wood siding and paneling 116; Shingles 117; Glossy solid colors 118;
    Wood flooring 119; Ceramic tile 120; Fabrics, upholstery, and carpet 121; Patterned wall covering 122

**Appendix  B:  MODEL  FURNITURE  DESIGNS**                                        123
    Club chair 124, Club sofa 124; Side chair 124; Conference or dining table 125; Dining chair 125;
    Coffee table 125; End table 126, Secretarial desk 126; Executive desk 126

**Appendix  C:  MARKER  COLOR  RECOMMENDATIONS**                                   127

**Appendix  D:  BUILDING  EXAMPLE  DESIGN  DRAWINGS**                              128

**INDEX**                                                                         135

# PREFACE

This project began as a comprehensive coverage of design and presentation media for design professionals of which modelbuilding was to be only one chapter. As I worked on this modelbuilding chapter, its length continued to expand to match my enthusiasm for the subject until it assumed the book form that you now hold.

This is not intended as a manual for professional modelbuilders. These specialists make extensive use of acrylic and other unconventional materials to literally machine model components to very close tolerances. While these techniques are efficient and yield beautifully crafted and detailed models, they require sophisticated equipment and specialized skills that are unfamiliar to most designers.

This book is intended instead as a guide for design professionals: architects, landscape architects, and interior designers. It focuses on techniques which are widely accepted within these professions...techniques which require a minimum of specialized skill and utilize readily available materials familiar to most designers.

In addition, I have tried to address the effectiveness of models as an active contributor in the schematic design process, and the potential of the process of constructing "presentation" models to provide the designer/ modelbuilder with ever greater insights into design development.

## Acknowledgments

A number of people have provided me with a great deal of assistance, advice, and encouragement in the preparation of this book. In particular, I want to thank Tom Briner, Gerardo Brown-Manrique, Virginia Cartwright, Bob Doran and Pat Moore of K. Z. F., Inc., Architects, Tom Dutton, Dan Enwright and Tamara Kenworthy of Space Design International, Richard Hill and Jim Ingram of I. P. G., Inc., Architects, Jeff Johnson of Charrette Corporation, Scott Johnston, Hayden May, Marietta Millet, John Taylor, and Robert Zwirn for the contributions that each has made to this book and my knowledge on the subject. Miami University has provided me with a fertile and supportive environment for not only teaching but also undertaking a project such as this. Finally, I owe a great debt to all of my former students who required me to seek clear and concise ways to articulate and demonstrate methods of modelbuilding.

Fuller Moore, 1990

# Chapter 1:
# INTRODUCTION

## THE DESIGN / PRESENTATION CONTINUUM

Models are often divided into two distinct categories: design study models and presentation models. This division is most distinct when the designer works with only the crudest model construction to aid in visualizing a design (intended for his or her use only). And once the design is finalized, it is then turned over to a "professional" modelbuilder (often outside the design office) to produce an object for marketing the project to the client or prospective occupants or lending institutions. This unfortunate division, if taken literally, is both artificial (in its separation of design and communication) and counterproductive. In practice, even the crudest design study models are "presented" to others, if only design associates. If this design model (no matter how schematic) is not crafted with some degree of care, it can be misleading in terms of scale, proportion, and connection.

And what better way to develop and refine a design than to have the "presentation" model constructed by the designer? Invariably, the very process of planning and fitting a miniature version of a building together will provide new insights and reveal alternatives. Even the most routine and repetitive modelbuilding tasks keep the designer "in contact" with the project and afford a fertile environment for considering design changes.

Yet, clearly, there is a difference in the character and use of models depending on when and why they are built. It is perhaps most convenient to think of the various model types as a continuum ranging from schematic study models through the presentation models intended primarily for outside parties.

## THE DESIGN STUDY MODEL,

at one end of this continuum, is a dynamic medium, created and constantly revised in the earliest stages of the design process for the purpose of giving the designer greater insight into the design as it emerges. It is essential that it be of a character and of materials that facilitate - even encourage - design changes. It is important that the design model be quickly buildable, because it is this very speed of construction that invites the designer to test the design in model form in the very earliest stages.

The needs for speed and changeability make the design model an apparently "unfinished" object, but they accomplish the intended purpose of helping the designer to visualize the design more completely. However, some designers are reluctant to show such a dynamic design representation to a client, either because of concern that such an unfinished appearance will appear somehow unprofessional to the client, or because of a reluctance to reveal design options still in a state of flux until they are more completely evaluated. Other designers prefer to use design models to actually involve the client in the active design process.

Whatever the role of the client with design models, such models are most valuable when they can be built quickly and relatively precisely with a minimum of technical skill; they are most effective when the designer is the modelbuilder.

### Chipboard...
has long been a favorite material for design models. It is inexpensive, has a has a pleasing neutral gray surface and core (which allows unobtrusive corner joints), and is easy to cut. For speed, it is often cut with scissors and assembled using tape or rubber cement.

### Clay...
is an excellent material for making small scale mass models during the design stage. It is especially suited for complex building and landscape forms. It was a favorite material of Louis I. Kahn, and it was used for client presentation models of some of his most famous projects. It should be an oil-based professional quality modeling clay that does not dry out and can thus be modified at any time. It is available in either a cream or green-gray color at art supply stores. Although special sculpting tools are available, for most architectural modeling a stylus made from a needle and a hobby knife are effective tools.

*Chipboard design model. (1/8" = 1'-0" [1:96] student project by N. Dixon.)*

*Clay and foam board design model on print of site aerial photograph. (KZF, Inc., Architects; 1:1000 model by J. Lichtenberg.)*

## Foam board...

is a sandwich of a sheet of polystyrene foam covered on each side with heavy white paper. It is useful for quickly cutting out the stories of a multistory building using a utility knife. Transfer plans as above. It is available in 3/16" (5 mm) thickness (use for single stories of 1" = 50' or 1:600 scale buildings) and 1/4" (6 mm) thickness (use for single stories of 1" = 40' or 1:800 scale buildings) at most art supply stores; available up to 1/2" (13 mm) thick in some locations.

## Polystyrene foam...

is a low-density white foam used for building insulation. It is available at lumberyards in 4' x 8' sheets (122 cm x 244 cm) in thicknesses of 1" (2.5 cm) and 2" (5 cm), and because it is typically manufactured in most large cities (to minimize shipping costs), it may be available in greater thicknesses. It can be cut smoothly using a hot-wire cutter (see description in Chapter 2). Because the considerable thickness of the foam can be cut so quickly using this technique, it is easy to sculpt building shapes. Compound curves such as domes and concave shapes are difficult to create and may require some hand shaping.

Foam board design model. (William Turnbull Associates / KZF, Inc., Architects; 1" = 40' [1:480] model by J. Hoster.)

## PRESENTATION    MODELS

At the other end of this continuum, presentation models are usually constructed only after most of the design decisions have been made.   In one sense, they are a record of the achievements of the design process. Yet, even these offer the designer the opportunity to visualize ever finer levels of design detail.   And they are the most literal, convincing, and realistic medium for communicating a proposed design to a client.

As any experienced designer knows, a floor plan is an abstract drawing that is very difficult for most clients to understand.   Elevations, axonometrics, and perspectives are increasingly pictorial representations that are more successful in communicating a project design.   But none of these compare with a model in terms of realism and visceral impact.   The model is the only medium that allows clients to project themselves into the design and, for the first time, realistically imagine what the proposed design will be like to inhabit.

## SCALE

The primary purpose of the presentation model largely determines the type of model used and the scale of construction.

**Large site models...**
are typically built at scales of 1" = 40' (1:800) and smaller. This scale range is selected where there are large site features that must be represented (such as roads, landforms, wooded areas, and adjacent buildings). Consequently, the small scale of the proposed building(s) necessitates showing only its overall form, with no facade details.

**Large building models...**
are usually built at scales between 1" = 30' (1:360) and 3/32" = 1'-0" (1:128). This scale range permits showing all of the major fenestration and exterior facade features and colors, as well as small areas of the surrounding site. At this scale, it is both difficult and undesirable to show facade details such as mullions, masonry coursing, joints, textures, and trim.

*Water front development master plan 1" = 100' (1:1200) site model (William Turnbull Associates, Architects).*

**Small building exteriors...**
such as houses are best modeled at
1/8" - 1'-0" (1:96).  This scale is
sufficiently large to show all exterior
design features (including materials
selection), yet it does not necessitate
showing the time-consuming minor details
required at larger scales.  Most
surface detail can be shown by
drawing shadows and joints (rather
than having them built up three-
dimensionally). Virtually all entourage
materials  (cars, trees, scale figures,
furniture) are readily available through
local sources or can be built with a
minimum of effort.

**Larger scales** (1/4" to 1/2" - 1-0" or
1:48 to 1:24) are only used for very
small building exteriors where small
decorative detail must be shown.
Although such detail is time-consuming to
create and necessitates that the three-
dimensional relief of the elevations be
built up rather than drawn on, it
allows showing detailed building textures
(such as wood grain) and small
ornamentation characteristic of
traditional designs.

**Detailed interior models...**
should be 3/8" scale (1:32) or larger to
show specific design features, including
furniture, finishes, and accessories.

*Interpretive nature center. (F. Moore,
Architect; 1/8" scale [1:96] model by S.
Johnston. )*

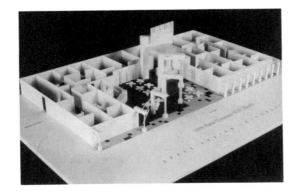

*Commercial exhibit booth. (Photo
courtesy of Space Design International;
1/8" scale [1:96] model by G.
Humphrey. )*

## Interior layout models...

are used for large areas where furniture is to be shown as abstract shapes for layout purposes only (typical scale range is 1/8" to 1/4" = 1'-0" or 1:48 to 1:24).

## Deciding coverage

If there are no factors to limit the physical size of the model, extend the base substantially beyond the building or immediate site in order to show the surrounding physical context. This is important in urban settings to show adjacent buildings and landscape features that affect the design. It is also important in rural locations to create a "natural" setting as well as showing site circulation features (walks, roads, parking) and the topography. Extending the base also improves the photographic potential of the model by allowing more foreground and background in "aerial" shots and a more realistic skyline for eye-level shots.

*Urban shading analysis. (Student project by S. Johnston.)*

## Physical size considerations

In planning the overall size of the model and base consider:

- Availability of display space (wall or floor mount?)

- Door widths (can the model be tilted on edge?)

- Shipping size limitations - U.S. Postal Service limitations are 70 lb, 108" length plus girth; United Parcel Service limitations are 70 lb (31.7 kg), 130" (330 cm) length plus girth.

- Transport limitations (standard station wagon and pickup truck widths = 48.25" or 122.5 cm).

- Size of locally available clear acrylic skylight domes if one is to be used as a protective display case.

## Interior visibility

For exterior models, the degree to which the interior will also be visible is an important planning consideration. Will the model show exterior only, interior only, or both (i.e., must the roof and/or upper floors be removable)? These factors are considered in detail in Chapter 6, Medium-Scale Building Models.

## OTHER MODEL TYPES

While this book is limited to a discussion of design and presentation models, there are several specialized model types suited for specific architectural applications, including photometric models for predicting daylight illumination in buildings (see Schiler, 1987; also Moore, 1985), models for analyzing the structural behavior of buildings (Cowan, H., et. al, 1968), "stage set" models for aiding in perspective construction (Burden, E., 1971), and cutaway models for demonstrating methods of construction.

Construction sequence. (Design and 1/8" scale [1:96] model by S. Johnston.)

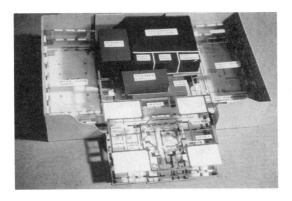

Multistory space utilization take-apart model of existing building. (Model by S. Johnston.)

Measuring daylight illumination in a model interior using multiple remote photometric sensors.

# Chapter 2:
# TOOLS AND SUPPLIES

It seems that every "how to" book contains an obligatory "Tools and Supplies" chapter. The tools and supplies for modelbuilding are remarkably simple and few. However, their design and quality are critical to achieving professional results within the time constraints of a typical office or academic environment.

## CUTTING TOOLS

### Utility Knife
Probably 95% of all modelbuilding cutting operations can best be done with the "utility" knife (a.k.a. matte knife). Its interchangeable blades are stiff and do not tend to "wander" on long straight cuts the way that "hobby" knives with thinner, more flexible blades do. The large handle fills the hand, is easier to control when pressure is applied for thick cuts, and is less fatiguing for long sessions. The blade-locking mechanism is positive and solid. The retractable version is preferable for reasons of safety; the rigidity of the blade mount is comparable to the nonretractable variety. These knives and replacement blades are available at hardware and art supply stores. The newer, heavy-duty utility knives with "break-off" blades are also suitable for heavy cutting, and they have the additional advantage of quicker blade replenishment. These segmented blades are replaceable, comparable in cost to a pack of five conventional double-ended blades, and somewhat less widely available.

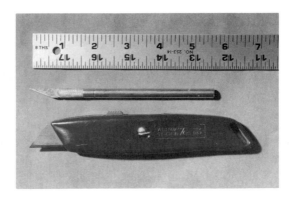

Utility knives, hobby knife, and straightedge.

## Hobby Knife

This popular type of knife should only be used for fine detail work where the long thin blade is an advantage. The blade is too thin for cutting illustration board because the blade bends under pressure and tends to "wander" away from the straightedge.

## Straightedge

Use a metal straightedge as a guide for making straight cuts. Impervious to nicks, it is more reliable and indestructible than plastic triangles (although the latter have the advantage of being transparent). Those made of stainless steel and 15" to 18" (40 mm to 50 mm) in length with a nonslip cork backing are best.

## Fine-toothed saw...

is used for cutting small pieces of wood (balsa and hardwood) in thicknesses greater than 1/16" (1.5 mm). When making cuts across the grain, knife blades tend to either tear or compress (and thus round) the edges of the work; the fine-toothed saw makes very clean crosscuts that require little or no sanding. They are available at hobby and art supply stores as auxiliary blades to fit heavy-duty hobby knife handles; buy the blade without the handle and use a wooden file handle.

Fine-toothed saw, coping saw, dressmaker's shears, embroidery scissors.

### The coping saw...

is useful for cutting out base contours from thick insulation board. The replaceable blades are thin and can cut very small radius curves. These blades can also be rotated to allow long cuts to be made by placing the saw frame off to the side.

### Scissors...

are useful in modelbuilding in two ways. First, large dressmaker's shears are useful for quick cutting of paper and thin illustration board, especially for curved cuts. Second, small embroidery scissors are helpful for making the forgotten cuts on illustration board pieces after they have been installed on a model. The opposing shearing action of the two blades allows cuts to be made without the destructive pressure required for in situ knife surgery.

## DRAFTING TOOLS

Most design professionals are familiar with the drafting tools useful for modelbuilding; the "archaic" ruling pen is indispensable for drafting with colored tempera.

Architectural and engineering scales, lead holder, technical pen, ruling pen, compass, adjustable triangle, and parallel bar.

# PAINTING TOOLS

## Lettering brushes

The preferred brush type for the application of small areas of tempera and latex paints (preferred for most modelbuilding applications) is the round red sable designed for brush lettering. When wet, this brush forms a square, knife-sharp chisel point that is superior to the more common conical watercolor shape for applying paint into rectangular areas with a minimum of brush marks.

Red sable is superior to other brush materials because, in spite of its very fine bristle tips, it is very resilient.

"Student" grade red sable lettering brushes are suitable for modelbuilding; the subtle qualities of the finer grades do not justify the difference in costs for this purpose. Three sizes are suggested: #2, #6, and #10.

**Caution:** Never use a red sable brush to apply any enamel or lacquer paint; it is virtually impossible to clean these paints out of the bristles completely enough for the brush to be satisfactory for water-based paints again. If latex paint is used, thoroughly clean the brush with water immediately after use. Latex paint dries quickly and, once dry, cannot be completely removed.

## Watercolor brushes

An economical alternative to red sable is the bamboo-handled watercolor brush. The bristles of these are softer and do not recover their shape the way red sable does; they are also more prone to shedding. After use, wash the paint out of the brushes immediately under running water by gently pinching the base of the bristles and "milking" the paint residue out to the end of the bristles. Using the fingers, shape the bristles into the optimum chisel shape and let the brush dry upside down (sitting handle-down in a jar, for example).

Red sable lettering brushes, bamboo-handle watercolor brush, nylon paintbrush, and disposable foam paintbrush.

### Paintbrushes

For applying large areas of latex paint on model bases, use the nylon bristle brushes recommended for this purpose that are available at most house paint supply and hardware stores. Use disposable foam brushes for applying any paint that will not clean up in water (i.e., all enamels, shellacs, lacquers, and oil-based paints) and throw away after use.

### The mouth atomizer...

is a useful tool for applying a coarse "spatter texture" spray over a large area or adding a "stippled" texture over a model base that has been painted with a base coat of latex. Mix the paint to be sprayed (tempera, watercolor, or latex) in a cup, thinning to the consistency of milk. Insert the long tube of the atomizer in the paint, and blow (hard) through the short end, aiming the nozzle somewhat above the target. For best results, spray two or more colors allowing time to dry in between. This is not recommended for solid coats, and it is not a substitute for an air brush or spray can which produce a much finer spray pattern.

### Spray paint...

in the form of an aerosol spray can is useful for coating large areas of delicate structures (a space frame, for example) where it is not practical to use a brush. However, spray cans are expensive to use, create overspray that must be controlled, are available in a limited range of colors, and clog easily. As a general rule, use spray cans only when brushes are not practical.

*Mouth atomizer.*

*Spatter texture created by tempera sprayed with mouth atomizer.*

## POWER TOOLS...

are not essential for modelbuilding; however, the following are convenient and can save some production time.

The **table saw** is useful for cutting plywood sheets into subbases, truing the sides of contour bases, mitering wood base trim, and occasional cutting hardwood model pieces.

The versatile 1/4" (6 mm) **power drill** is useful for a wide variety of tasks because of the numerous accessories available. Recommended are metal bits (1/16", 1/8", 3/16", and 1/4" or 1.5 mm, 3 mm, 5 mm, and 6 mm sizes), wood bits (3/8", 1/2", 3/4", and 1" or 10 mm, 13 mm, 19 mm, and 25 mm), screwdriver bits (slotted and phillips), and sanding disk.

The **sabre saw** is useful for cutting 1/2" (13 mm) insulation board for model contours, although a coping saw can be used for this operation quite satisfactorily (and nearly as fast - insulation board is very easy to cut).

The principal advantage of the sabre saw is that it is easier to make an exactly vertical cut than is possible with a hand-held coping saw (however, in practice, this precision is not particularly critical to the appearance of the base). Buy extra blades with the finest tooth available.

A **hot-wire cutter** can be used to quickly shape blocks of polystyrene for mass and site models. The thin hot wire makes a smooth cut even through thick blocks of foam. Commercial models are available with adjustments that allow the wire to be tilted and foot-pedal controls.

These can be home-made using fine nichrome wire (see Charrette, 1989) connected to a variable voltage transformer; use a spring to maintain constant tension on the wire and a foot switch for convenient cutoff. Because the fumes from the melting polystyrene are both obnoxious and toxic, use these cutters only in a well-vented area.

Hot-wire cutter. (Photo courtesy of Charrette, Inc.)

## SUPPLIES

### Subbase Materials

Wood product sheet materials available at lumberyards make the best subbase materials. Plywood and its less expensive substitutes, flake board and particleboard (not to be confused with gray "chipboard," which is a paper board), are available in 4' x 8' (122 mm x 244 mm) size in thicknesses from 1/4" to 3/4" (6 to 18 mm) in 1/8" (3 mm) increments. Because the most important quality of the subbase is resistance to bending and warping, the 3/4" (19 mm) thickness is recommended for bases with any dimension larger than 24" (60 cm).

### Plywood...

can be interior type, in surface grades of C or D (the smoother and more expensive A and B grades are unnecessary as all of the subbase is covered). For large bases, consider using all or part of a 1 3/4" (44 mm) thick hollow-core, flush-face door. The honeycomb construction of these makes them comparatively light in weight and resistant to warping. The least expensive ones have a hardboard face which is acceptable for subbase. Ask about the availability of damaged doors at a reduced price; these also make excellent drafting table tops.

### Wood-fiber insulating or sheathing board...

is available at lumberyards in 4' x 8' x 1/2" thickness (122 cm x 244 cm x 13 mm). This material is known by various names in different localities and has slightly different surface characteristics depending on the local application. All consist of a low-density, compressed wood fiber material that is light tan in color. Today, it is most widely available as an interior "insulating board," often with a white paint finish on one side (tan core and back). The tan core and "back" are the essential characteristics for this material to be used as contours as both the core and the back are exposed in the finished model.

Another version is used as an exterior wall sheathing material (applied under finish siding). The only contemporary version of this wall sheathing available locally may be impregnated with asphalt (dark brown to black throughout the entire thickness), which is not suitable for model applications.

## White-core illustration board

The most versatile material for modelbuilding is a high-quality, five-ply (approximately 1/20" or 1 mm thick), 100% rag, cold-pressed illustration board (such as manufactured by Strathmore). It is "the" preferred material for most flat building model surfaces. The white cold-pressed surface has a medium "tooth" which allows it to take pencil and marker color as well as drafting ink. Both sides are identical and can be used as finished surfaces; this symmetry also reduces warping. Most important, the core of this board is also white, allowing the edges to be colored or left white to match the surface. This allows the use of butt joints which are easy to create and all but invisible, instead of the more difficult miter joint. The comparatively high cost of this particular type of illustration board is more than compensated by the time saved in finishing the joints. Furthermore, since this one board can be used to create a wide range of colors and textures, it minimizes the necessity of "stocking" a large inventory of different board types. A similar white "board" which is available in one and two plies is used for single-curved surfaces and for laminating a finished surface over a substrate.

### "Chipboard"...

is a gray cardboard used for the preliminary building of mass models and topographic contours. The warm gray color is neutral and pleasing in appearance. It is even used by many designers as a presentation model material, taking advantage of the slightly different gray colors on each side to create contrasts between different model surfaces. Chipboard is available in 1/24" (1 mm - single) thickness and 1/12" (2 mm - double) thickness.

### Other illustration boards...

are available in a wide variety of textures, colors, and patterns. In general, these should only used where a large uniform area of colored texture is required (for example, a large expanse of level lawn area). Such boards are difficult to use for modeling three-dimensional objects because of the contrast between the colored surface and the gray core that shows at corners. In most cases, the above white board is used instead, being colored and textured as required for the specific application.

### Foam...

materials are available that can be used for simple mass models. All can be cut using the hot-wire cutter described above in a well-ventilated location. Glue with white glue. Many foams cannot be conveniently painted.

Expanded polystyrene (beadboard) is inexpensive and available from the local lumberyard. It is white and cuts readily leaving a smooth finish. It is, however, very soft and cannot withstand handling. It can be painted with latex paint.

Extruded polystyrene is usually available locally only in light blue. It cuts easily and leaves an open-grained surface. Its texture is firmer than beadboard but still not suitable for public handling. Paint with latex.

Polyethylene foam is open-grained and more flexible than extruded polystyrene. Available from model suppliers (see Charrette, 1989) in white and black, it accepts enamels, markers, and contact cement.  It is well suited for models and mock-ups which see hard use.

High-density polystyrene foam is available from model suppliers (see Charrette, 1989) in white.  It yields clean hard surfaces when cut with a hot-wire cutter, is sandable, and is suitable for presentation models.

Polyurethane foam is another premium quality material particularly well suited for modelbuilders. It is often routed by specialty model base fabricators to form topographic contours.

Expanded polyvinyl-chloride (PVC) is available from model suppliers (see Charrette, 1989) in white and black. It can be stapled, nailed,  riveted, knife- or saw-cut, glued, and painted.

Sheet acrylic is rigid and virtually flat and is ideal for simulating glass.  In 1/32" (0.8 mm) thickness, it can still be cut easily with a knife and can be glued with either "super glue" or plastic model cement.  Unfortunately, the 1/32" thickness is seldom available through conventional local sources; order directly from model suppliers (see Charrette, 1989).

The clear variety can also be used as an invisible "base" for drawing to simulate railing balusters and ornamental details (see the description in Chapter 5). In addition to the clear variety, this thickness is also available in gray and mirror-backed, the latter being ideal for simulating mirrors on interior models and mirror-surfaced building materials.

Clear vinyl or acetate sheet is readily available locally in the form of plastic report covers available at stationery stores. It is very flexible and is only a satisfactory substitute for the stiffer sheet acrylic (above) for simulating glass for small windows that are surrounded by supporting wall material. The ripples that are inevitable for larger areas cause such distortion in the reflections that the illusion of glass is completely lost. The flexibility of this material can be an advantage if the glazing is curved; when flexed into a cylindrical shape and constrained at each end, it gains the rigidity necessary to produce realistic reflections.

Clear contact vinyl sheets are pressure-sensitive films used to overlay matte finish illustration board to give either a high gloss (laminating plastic; available in stationery and art supply stores) or semigloss (contact vinyl covering, available in rolls in various patterns and colors as well as clear; available in hardware and discount department stores). They are superior to spray applications.

Clear pressure-sensitive vinyl sheet for adding semigloss finish..

# ADHESIVES

## White glue...

may be used for 95% of all model-gluing operations on paper, illustration board, and wood.  It dries moderately fast, allowing just about the right amount of time for positioning and adjusting pieces.  It is inconspicuous, drying semimatte and clear.  Buy it by the quart and use it to refill easy-to-handle 4-oz squeeze bottles.  Refill before the small bottle is half empty to minimize the wait for the glue to drain to the spout at the beginning of each gluing sequence.

## Spray adhesive...

is a convenient method of laminating paper onto a substrate.  Spray a thin coating onto both contacting surfaces and let it dry.  Be careful in positioning the paper initially; this adhesive creates a permanent bond on contact, so there is virtually no opportunity to reposition or eliminate wrinkles.  For larger areas it is helpful to place an "interleaf" sheet of tracing paper between the two surfaces to prevent premature adhesion.  After positioning the top paper, slide the interleaf out an inch (a couple centimeters) at a time, progressively rubbing down the top paper in the newly exposed strip of adhesive.

**Caution:** This is a very messy material and the overspray is virtually impossible to remove from model surfaces - and floors and furniture.  Use it outside, or inside only with carefully prepared protection for overspray.  Finally, because the fumes are at least obnoxious (and often toxic), use spray adhesive only in a well-vented area.

**Hot glue guns** are not recommended because they simply cannot be controlled well enough for any but the crudest modelbuilding operations.  The resulting joints are weak in comparison with conventional glues.  And they can cause serious burns when the melted glue inevitably drips on the skin.

## WOOD STRIPS

Use **balsa** wood for square columns, mullions, and miscellaneous model shapes. Balsa can be either painted (with tempera) or stained (with marker). It is also useful as a structural stiffener for long expanses of illustration board. Balsa is available at most art supply and hobby stores in various rectangular shapes in lengths of 36" (90 cm). If available, **basswood** is superior to balsa for most architectural modelbuilding operations because its denser grain allows it to hold detail better and makes finishing easier. Basswood is available in shapes that simulate structural steel as well as rectangular shapes, in lengths of 24" (60 cm). It is usually available in art supply stores or through mail-order suppliers (see Charrette, 1989).

**Dowels** are round hardwood (usually maple) sticks 36" (91 mm) long in diameters from 1/8" (3 mm) up to 1" (25 mm). The are useful for round columns, tree bases, railings, etc., and can be found locally at art supply stores, as well as lumberyards.

# COATINGS AND RENDERING MATERIALS

## Markers...

are felt-tip applicators with a wide palette of alcohol-based colors. These are "the" preferred coloring medium (on white illustration board) for the building model. They are available in a wide range of colors at art supply stores. They are ready for use with no preparation, and they dry instantly.

They are easy to apply using a straightedge as a guide, and depending on the spacing of the strokes, the darker "overlay" area can be used to advantage in simulating the color variation inherent in building materials. Finally, markers do not warp illustration board or paper; this is a major advantage over virtually all paint-type coloring materials which cause unacceptable warping of these materials. They are also excellent for staining balsa and basswood, allowing the grain to remain visible. See Appendix C for marker colors recommended for rendering various building materials. Some markers have two tip sizes: a fine point at one end and a broader point at the other. The broad width is usually used for covering broad areas, usually with a straightedge to make the streaking more uniform. The fine tip is occasionally used for detail and darkening shadows under convex areas (such as stones).

The disadvantages of markers are their comparatively high cost (in a professional office environment, the savings in time will more than compensate this), their lack of "correctability" (mistakes are corrected by gluing on a layer of white paper), their lack of permanence (they tend to fade after long exposure to strong light), and their transparency (the effects of the materials below "bleed" through; of course, this can also be considered one of the advantages of markers).

Felt-tip markers.

## Pastels...

are soft colored chalk, recommended for application on white illustration board. They are available in a very wide color range and are easy to apply over large areas. Grind a powder from the pastel stick using sandpaper, and dab the powder with a cotton ball and smear it onto the illustration board.

For more intense color, apply the pastel stick directly to the illustration board and smooth it with a finger or cotton. Remove excess powder with a drafting brush. Pastel erases readily and completely; the preferred technique is to smear it on and erase the unwanted areas with the aid of an erasing shield. After all erasing is done, make the pastel area permanent by spraying it with a workable fixative (or hair spray).

## Ink...

applied with a technical drawing pen, is the recommended medium for linework on a model surface (for example, siding shadow lines, roof shingles, or brick coursing). Providing that waterproof ink is used, draw details using the pen on white illustration board prior to overcoating with transparent color (such as markers, pastels, or watercolor). Test to make sure that the ink will not smear when overcoated. If any smearing occurs, coat with color first and then apply the inkwork; however, light pencil layout lines will be more difficult to see through the applied color.

Cotton application of pastels.

### Graphite pencil...

in addition to its use as a layout medium, is a useful rendering medium for applying linework and textures to illustration board (when black ink linework would result in too much contrast) or when a softer, more freehand quality is desired. Pencil can be applied either before (less contrast) or after (more contrast) the coloring medium is applied.

### Colored pencil...

can be used for coloring small areas or where colored linework is be added. It is difficult to apply uniformly over a large area. Applied over a "medium-tooth" white illustration board, it accentuates the grainy texture of the surface. It is opaque and tends to cover previous applications. Use only artist-quality pencils (such as Berol Prismacolor) which are available in a wide range of colors. Because these pencils are comparatively soft, they dull quickly, making it difficult to achieve thin, crisp colored lines (see Tempera).

### Tempera...

is an opaque water-based and water-soluble paint that dries to a matte finish. Applied with a ruling pen, tempera is ideal for making straight, crisp colored lines that completely cover any underlying medium.

As the tempera in the ruling pen begins to dry, clogging will occur. Unclog the pen by inserting a folded piece of paper towel between the two nibs of the pen and pull the towel down through the paint reservoir area and out the tip. Refill with fresh tempera using a brush and continue drafting.

Drawing colored lines using tempera and a ruling pen.

Tempera can be used to "paint" small areas, but it is not recommended for application on large areas of illustration board because it will cause warping. It is ideal for painting small objects, such as furniture and vehicles. It is an inexpensive medium available in small jars in the primary colors, white, and black. These are well-suited for the above application.

**Designer's colors...**

are similar to tempera but are a more intense and finely ground medium. They come in tubes in a wider range of colors, are more expensive, and generally are not needed for modelbuilding applications.

**Watercolor...**

is a transparent, water-based, waterproof (after drying) medium. Because of its tendency to warp illustration board, it is not recommended for modelbuilding.

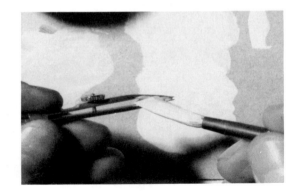

Filling the ruling pen using a brush.

### Shellac...

is an alcohol-based primer that is an excellent sealer (allowing water-based paints to be applied over paper and illustration board without warping) for contoured model bases to be painted. It dries almost instantly and can be immediately recoated with the finish paint. Available as either "orange" or "clear" shellac, both are satisfactory as a primer for opaque paint. Buy it in 8-oz or larger cans at the local paint or hardware store. The high cost of the alcohol solvent makes cleaning brushes impractical; use disposable foam brushes.

### Latex spackling compound...

is a remarkable material, an excellent, nonshrinking filler that dries almost instantly. It is used for filling cracks and creating fillets (rounding interior corners). It dries flat white and is great for hiding defects on white illustration board models. Apply with the fingers or a knife blade. Clean up immediately with a damp cloth or tissue (like latex paint, it is water-soluble only before it dries). It can be painted over within a few minutes of application. Buy a small (4-oz) cup at the hardware store.

### Latex paint

Once dry, latex paint is insoluble, making this opaque coating excellent for large areas where subsequent overpainting in a different color will be required (for example, contoured model bases to be overpainted with roads and walks). Prime first with shellac. Apply the latex paint with a brush as it comes from the can; its thick consistency hides defects and dries to a smooth, matte finish. One coat is usually sufficient. It can be purchased in quarts (and larger) in virtually any color premixed at the local hardware or paint supply center. Either latex or acrylic latex is suitable, provided it will dry to a matte (flat) finish.

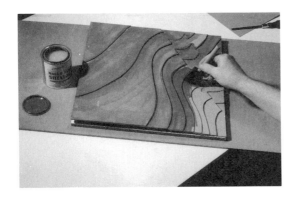

Sealing the contours with shellac.

Apply latex spackling compound to fill the joints.

Painting the model base with latex enamel.

Buy a quart of light gray-green to simulate grass; select a considerably lighter and grayer color chip than might be expected (it will seem more intense and darker when applied over the large area of the base). If many "urban" models with large areas of paving are anticipated, buy a second quart of white that can be mixed with small amounts of tempera to create various paving grays, etc. **Hint:** When mixing grays, black added to white latex results in an unattractive cool gray; warm it up by adding a little brown tempera.

**Plaster of paris...**
is mixed with water for casting objects (such as model cars). Add water while stirring until it has the consistency of heavy cream. Pour immediately into the mold, and allow to dry overnight before sanding and painting. It is available in small quantities at hardware and art supply stores.

# Chapter 3:
# THE MODEL BASE

## SUBBASE

The first step in model construction is the fabrication of a subbase. This is a stiff, boardlike material upon which the topographic base (and the rest of the model) is constructed. While it is likely that the subbase will ultimately be concealed from view, it is an important component because it is the structural foundation of the model. As such, the subbase should be sufficiently stiff to prevent any future warping. Warping can, at the least, cause a distortion of the appearance of the base; at the worst, it can damage the building model itself. A second criterion of the subbase is its workability; it should be both nailable and gluable.

For smaller subbases (up to 2' or 60 cm square) use a 1/2" (13 mm) thick material such as plywood, wood particleboard, or wood fiber wall sheathing. All of these are available at local lumberyards. Most types of illustration board, including board with a foam core, are unacceptable for even this small base size as they will warp with changes in humidity and temperature.

For larger subbases even stiffer materials such as 3/4" (19 mm) plywood and particleboard should be used. Hollow-core, flush-face doors make an excellent lightweight, stiff model subbase for larger size models. Thin plywood which has been edge-stiffened (with, for example, 1 x 2's or 2 cm x 4 cm) is not satisfactory. While it is lightweight and will resist bending, it is still prone to twisting.

## ENLARGING THE SITE PLAN

Once the scale of the model has been determined, the site plan must be enlarged (or reduced) to this scale. Whatever the method of enlargement, begin by drawing a graphic scale reference directly on the original site plan. For example, draw a line to scale the length of which is equal to 50' (or, say, 10 meters); later, in the process of enlarging the site plan, this graphic scale will provide an accurate indicator of the degree of enlargement needed.

### The opaque projector...

provides a convenient method of enlarging a site plan. Place the original site plan in the projector and project its enlarged image onto a wall-mounted sheet of heavy tracing paper in a darkened room. Adjust the distance of the projector to the wall so that when the image is focused, the size of the projected graphic scale line is the correct size.

Determine this by measuring the projected line with an engineering (or architectural) scale that corresponds to the chosen scale of the model base. This is a trial-and-error process; each time the projector is moved to change

the scale, it must be refocused and the refocusing process itself changes the magnification. It is important that the projection be made perpendicular to the wall to avoid any perspective (or "keystone"-shaped) distortion of the projected site plan. For most model bases, a small amount of distortion here is not critical. However, if the site plan includes elements the shape of which must be preserved exactly, lay out a reference square on the original site plan and make sure that this image is projected as square. To correct keystone distortion, tilt the projection angle. Once the projected image is satisfactory, trace it onto the tracing paper using a pencil.

## Photocopy enlarging

If the size of the original site plan is sufficiently small and a photocopier with a variable enlargement capability is available, this method may be used. Make enlarged and reenlarged copies of the original until the proper scale is achieved. The graphic scale drawn on the original site plan is used to determine the final enlargement. Again, this is a trial-and-error process. It may be necessary to enlarge the site plan in sections to be later assembled using tape.

One disadvantage of this method is that some enlarging photocopiers produce a slightly different degree of enlargement of the vertical and horizontal axes, resulting in a slightly "stretched" appearance. This effect is usually minimal, resulting in a 2 or 3% distortion of the final image after several enlarging iterations. Again, this distortion can be measured by employing a reference square drawn on the original site plan and comparing the height and width after enlargement. For most presentation model bases, this amount of distortion is unnoticeable.

## Photographic projection...

is a convenient method of enlargement for large site plans (which exceed the capacity of opaque projectors or photocopiers). Photograph the original site plan using a 35 mm camera with slide or negative film. After processing, place the mounted image in a slide projector. The enlargement process is similar to that described for opaque projection above. It is important to photograph the original site plan from a perpendicular location (the film plane should be parallel to the site plan) if distortion is to be avoided. Similarly, the image should be projected at a perpendicular angle for the same reason. As with the opaque projector method, use a graphic scale and a square drawn on the original site plan to control enlargement and distortion of the final image.

## Manual grid enlargement

For those who have never done a manual grid enlargement, this process sounds prohibitively time consuming. In practice, after the first few squares, the process goes quickly, and even a large site plan with complex contours can be enlarged in an hour or so. Unless the proper enlargement equipment is conveniently available, manual grid enlargement may be the most convenient method, especially for reasonably simple site plans.

Begin by drawing a square grid over the entire site plan at some convenient size (for example, one grid square equals a 25' or a 10 m square). On a new sheet of heavy tracing paper, draw a corresponding grid at the scale of the model base. For ease of reference, designate the rows and columns of the original and new grids in an identical manner. For example, number the rows consecutively (1, 2, 3, etc.) and letter the columns in a like manner (A,B,C, etc.). The original site plan has been subdivided by the grid into a number of smaller, simple "sites." In each corresponding square on the new sheet, sketch freehand the site features from each grid of the original site plan.

# BASE TOPOGRAPHY

## Level sites

If the proposed site is level (or nearly so), preparing the model base is simply a process of rendering the site plan onto a sheet of illustration board which is then glued to a subbase. A simple method for preparing such a base is to select a sheet of matte finish illustration board in the color of the predominant ground cover material. For example, use a matte-finish gray-green illustration board if the site is predominantly covered with grass.   Indicate additional landscape elements using any of a variety of rendering mediums, including tempera, watercolor, pastels, colored pencils, or colored charcoal paper cutouts applied with rubber cement.

On such level sites, if the location is either urban or suburban, the three-dimensional relief of curbs can be used to emphasize the difference between streets and other site areas.   This can be done by fabricating the base in two layers.   The first layer is a sheet of illustration board that covers the entire subbase in a color to simulate street paving material. The second layer is a sheet of illustration board in the predominant color of the remaining site with the street areas cut out and removed.

## Simple, nonlevel topography

If the site is not level but its shape is simple (for example, flat but tilted or simple, single-curved slopes), then sheet illustration board glued to the top of appropriately profiled supports can be used to represent the site topography. Even site plans with irregular topographic contours can often be simplified in order to use this method for presentation models.

Begin with a scale drawing showing the section profile through the site. Use this profile to cut a series of identical profile supports out of thin gray chipboard.   Cut enough of these profile supports so that they can be arranged on the subbase parallel to one another at a spacing of no more than 3" (about 10 cm) apart in order to give sufficient support to the top layer. Edge-glue these to the subbase using white glue. Position the first and last profile support about 1/4" (6 mm) in from the edge of the subbase to allow for future trimming of the assembled base using a table saw. Give lateral support to the profile strips by gluing on small perpendicular chipboard squares.

Cut and glue in some vertical strips of chipboard at each end of the model; these are perpendicular to (and the same height as) the profile strips. The

purpose of these end pieces is to provide additional support for the end edge of the top cover between the profile strips at each end. Again, these should be kept about 1/4" (6 mm) from the edge of the subbase to allow for trimming.

If the top of the profile strips is curved (in order to create a curved, sloping topography), then the curved shape of the top sheet will provide an inherent stiffness. However, if there are large flat areas, it may be necessary to provide additional support between the profile supports by installing some perpendicular cross pieces of the same height.

Cut out a sheet of board to be used for the final base surface the same size as the subbase. Apply glue to the top of all of the vertical support pieces and position the top sheet in place. Apply temporary weights as necessary to make the top sheet conform to the shape of the supports while the glue is drying.

If a second layer is to be used to represent curbs, then apply this precut sheet in the same manner.

Once the glue is dry, trim the four sides of the base using a table saw. Make these cuts slowly to prevent tearing the top cover sheet. This

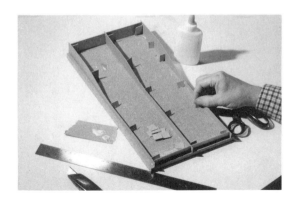

Edge-glue "section" profile strips onto base.

Apply weights to the top board to conform it to the shape of the section profile strips while glue dries.

Base after edge strips are applied and trimmed.

trimming will ensure that the sides of both the subbase and the top cover are exactly perpendicular and will greatly simplify the next step of fitting a covering trim to the sides of the base. To cover the exposed edges of the base, stand the base on its edge and trace around its outline onto a piece of illustration or chipboard. Cut out this piece leaving one end long for later trimming. Repeat this for the remaining sides. Glue these edge-trim pieces on around the model base in a pinwheel manner leaving the extended ends overhanging. Once the glue is dry, trim off the excess lengths using a utility knife.

## Complex topography

More complex landforms are usually represented with topographic contours. On the site plan, the curved topographic contours represent lines of equal height (elevation) on the surface of the site. For example, the 108' (or 33 m) contour shows the locations on the site that are 108' (33 m) above some predetermined reference level (i.e., sea level).

If the contours are spaced widely on the site plan, then the slope of the site is shallow (i.e., there is a large distance between 1' [30 cm] differences in height on the site). Conversely, closely spaced contours represent a

steep slope. The slope of the contours is always exactly perpendicular to the contours; i.e., after a rainfall, the runoff would always be downhill - perpendicular to the contours.

On the site plan, contours are a convenient way to represent the three-dimensional form of a site on a two-dimensional drawing. On the model base, the contours must be translated into the three-dimensional form that they represent. In order to do this, it is first necessary to know the "interval" of the contours. In other words, do the contours represent one foot (30 cm) differences in elevation (one foot contour interval) or some larger vertical spacing? Site plan contours are numbered according to their elevation; the contour interval is the numerical difference between two adjacent contours.

For anything other than large area site plans (where the model is to be constructed at a very small scale) a 1' (25 cm) contour interval should be used. If the site plan shows contours of a greater interval, then they must be "interpolated" by sketching in the additional necessary contours, equally spaced between the originals. Once a site plan with contours is completed, it should be drawn onto a sheet of heavyweight tracing paper.

In the final model base, these contours will appear as high "steps." These steps will form a somewhat abstract representation of a smoothly undulating natural landscape. Under normal circumstances, site plan contours will never cross. In the case where there is a vertical retaining wall, it is conventional for several contours to converge and "stack up" on top of one another.

It is usually easier to build the base and the contours to fit around the building than it is to try to fit the building down on top of the contours. Therefore, lay out the contours as though they continued through the

building area uninterrupted; once the building model is constructed and accurately outlined on the base, it is a simple operation to cut out the "building" contours to allow the building to be recessed into the base.

Flip the working site tracing over. Using a very soft graphite pencil "scribble" a wide line following each contour. This graphite backing will convert the tracing sheet into a "carbon" paper. Flip the tracing back over so that the right side is up, and position it over the base material which has been cut out to the size of the model subbase. Attach the tracing using pushpins and, using a ballpoint pen, retrace the

Lay out contours on a large sheet of paper.

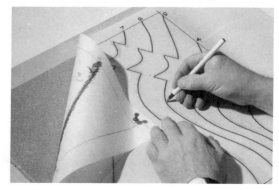

After applying graphite to the back of the contour paper, trace over the contours to transfer them onto the sheet of contour material below.

contours using a light pressure to transfer the graphite backing onto the base material.

There are a variety of different methods for fabricating a contoured model base. The following are efficient techniques that will cover most modelbuilding situations and yet require a minimum of special equipment or materials.

### "Slipped sheathing" contours

For this method use a sheet of 1/2" (13 mm) wood-fiber sheathing. Begin the base by cutting out two pieces of sheathing material the size of the base. Transfer the contours to the tan side of each of these pieces. One of these will be used for the subbase. If the model is to be larger than 3' (1 m) square, then substitute a stiffer material for the subbase. The contour outline on this subbase will provide a convenient reference for positioning contour pieces. Using a coping saw, cut out each of the contours from the second piece. Number each contour piece, beginning with #1 for the lowest.

For models of this size (less than 3' square), the coping saw is sufficient and even preferable to a power sabre saw. The coping saw cuts through this low-density material very quickly with a minimum of effort. Furthermore, the narrow coping saw blade allows much smaller turns than are possible with a power saw. Save all of the sawdust from this cutting operation; it will be used as a filler material later in the process.

To prepare the supports for the cutout contours, begin by ruling a set of parallel lines on a sheet of thin chipboard. Make the first two lines 1/2" (13 mm) apart; this will become a

Using a coping (or sabre) saw, cut out every contour line and save the sawdust.

Lay out and cut progressively wider strips of chipboard to be used as contour supports.

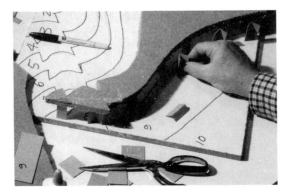

Glue the L-shaped supports onto the subbase, and install the contour section, taking care to align it over the contour outline on the subbase.

1/2"-wide strip that will be cut into pieces to form 1/2"-high supports for the first (lowest) contour section.

Assuming that the contour interval is 1' (30 cm), and the scale is 1/8" = 1'-0" (1:96), then the support for the next highest contour should be 1/8" (3 mm) taller than the last. Therefore, draw another parallel line, this time 5/8" (16 mm) below the last. Number this strip #2. Repeat the process drawing several parallel lines, each 1/8" (3 mm) further apart than the last; number all of these consecutively. Using a metal straightedge and a utility knife (with a cutting board underneath), cut this chipboard into strips.

Beginning with the largest (i.e., least bendable) contour section that was previously cut, cross-cut the corresponding chipboard strip into rectangular pieces about 3/4" (19 mm) long. Fold each piece to form L-shaped angle pieces the height of each of which is equal to the width of the original strip.

Squeeze out a small puddle of white glue onto a scrap piece of chipboard, dip the end of each of these supports, and position them on the subbase in the corresponding area for that contour piece. Next, apply glue to the top of each of these supports and position the contour piece on the top. Check to

make sure that the contour is resting on each of the supports; if necessary, add some temporary weights to the top of the contour while the glue is drying.

Repeat the same process for the adjacent contour. Prior to installing this contour, run a bead of glue along the edge of the contour so that this piece is glued to the edge of the previously installed contour as well as all of the supports underneath.

Insert each of the remaining contour sections in the same manner. When all of these are in place, run a thin bead along the crack between each contour piece. While this glue is still wet,

After gluing the next set of supports to the subbase, edge-glue the next contour section to the previous one.

After all sections have been assembled, apply a thin bead of glue along the joints.

"Smear" on the sawdust, working it into the joints.

spread on the previously collected sawdust. Dust off the excess immediately, and the result is an apparently seamless, monolithic contour block.

In selecting tan insulating sheathing, it was assumed that this tan would be left natural as the primary base color. If some color differentiation is desired for a paved area (for example), this can be achieved in a variety of ways, including brush painting and spraying. For small areas, add color using a dark colored pencil.

Once the coloring of the base is complete, then trim the base on a table saw to even up the sides of the contours and the subbase so that they are perpendicular to the bottom.
Set the base on its edge on top of a piece of gray chipboard (or colored illustration board) and scribe the profile of the contours using a pencil. Cut out each of these side pieces and glue them around the base in a pinwheel fashion as illustrated. Once the glue is dry, trim the pinwheel extensions flush to complete the model base.

**Spaced chipboard contours**
Begin by cutting out two sheets of thin chipboard the size of the subbase. Using the tracing contour sheet, transfer all of the contours to the first sheet, drawing the even-numbered contours as continuous lines and the odd-numbered contours as solid lines. Repeat the process for the second sheet, this time showing the even contours dashed and the odd ones solid. Using a light pencil, number each piece according to the number of the dashed contour line on that piece. Cut out each solid contour line on each sheet.

After drying, the result is a seamless contour block.

Apply the edge strips in "pinwheel" pattern using masking tape to temporarily hold them into place while the glue dries.

Trim ends after drying and the base is complete.

Glue the lowest numbered contour directly onto the subbase. Cut up an ample supply of small chipboard squares to be used as spacer blocks. Notice that the thin chipboard is not thick enough to represent the full contour thickness and therefore requires one or two spacers between each chipboard contour layer. The thickness of the chipboard contour piece combined with the thickness of these spacers should equal the scaled height of the contour.

Glue spacers onto the top of the first contour piece just inside of the dotted line; since the dotted line represents the edge of the next contour, this will ensure that the spacers are concealed. Build up several additional spacer stacks to the same height to support the back edge of the contour. Repeat the process for the second and each subsequent contour. After about the third or fourth contour, it may be more efficient to cut out vertical L-shaped supports instead of stacking up more and more spacers.

Trim the edges of the base using a table saw. Scribe, cut, and apply the finishing edge-trim pieces in the manner shown above.

**Finished chipboard contours**
Begin with two pieces of thick gray chipboard cut to the size of the subbase. The thickness of the chipboard should be equal to the contour interval. (Check this by counting the number of sheets in a 1" stack.) Transfer the contours to the subbase and to both sheets of chipboard. Cut out the even-numbered contours on one sheet and the odd-numbered ones on the other (in the manner described above).

Glue the lowest numbered contour directly onto the subbase. Cut up a supply of 1/2" square spacers from the same thickness chipboard. At a

Trace and cut even- and odd-numbered contours on different sheets of contour material.

Using chipboard square spacers to support the next highest contour, measure and cut vertical L-shaped supports for taller heights.

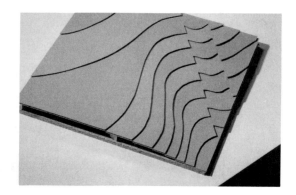

Finished spaced-contour base.

spacing of about 2" (5 cm), glue spacer pieces onto the base to support the next contour piece. Repeat the process for the second and subsequent contours.

Coat the assembled base with shellac in order to seal it to prevent warping when water-based paint is applied later. Clear shellac is available at most hardware stores and (being alcohol-based) dries very quickly. Apply using a disposable foam brush because the task of cleaning shellac out of a brush consumes more alcohol thinner than the brush is worth.

Using latex-based spackling compound (available at most hardware stores), smooth the "step" between the contours using a finger to squeegee the paste into the crack to form a concave fillet. Wipe off any excess immediately with a damp paper towel because this plaster dries very quickly. To get a smooth finish after filling the joints, lightly wipe over the fillets again with a moistened finger. Let this dry for 10 or 15 min.

For the final coat, latex base paint is preferable because it is easy to apply without brush marks, it dries matte and waterproof (and therefore can be overcoated with a different color),

and it can be cleaned up with water before it dries. Have the local hardware store mix up a quart of gray-green house paint. Typically, the minimum quantity is a quart, which will be sufficient for several bases. There is a tendency to select a color from a chart in the store that ultimately appears too bright when applied to a model base. **Select** a color that appears right, but **buy** the color that is midway between the selection and a neutral gray.

Coat the entire top of the model base with this latex paint and allow it to dry (15 to 30 min). If necessary, apply a second coat to get solid coverage.

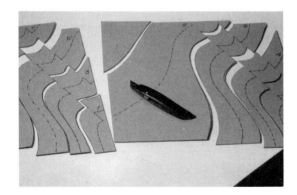

Trace and cut even- and odd-numbered contours on different sheets of contour material (thickness equal to one contour interval).

Transfer the contours onto the subbase. Glue the contours into place, using chipboard spacer squares to support the back of the contours.

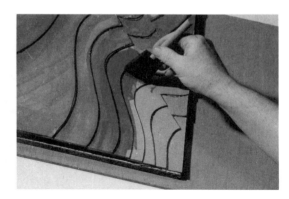

Seal the contours with a coat of shellac.

While the base coat is drying, pour out a couple ounces of the green latex paint and add some red tempera in order to mix a gray paving color. Once the base coat is dry, mask out the edges of the paving with masking tape (apply only light pressure to prevent the tape from lifting the base paint) and apply the road color with a brush. Immediately (but carefully) strip off the masking tape and, if necessary, do any touch-up at that time.

These latex paints dry quite uniformly, but unfortunately they have no texture resulting in a bland appearance. To apply a lightly sprayed texture to the base, mix up some water-based colors

(tempera, for example). It is suggested that one color should be the same as the road, another a muted brown, and another a light tan. Thin to a milklike consistency.

Use a mouth atomizer (or a toothbrush dipped in paint and rubbed over a piece of screen wire) to spray a light spatter of each of these colors. Allow a couple minutes for drying between each color to prevent the droplets from running together. The resulting base is richly textured and has a very realistic appearance.

Once all painting operations are complete, trim the base using a table

saw. Scribe and apply the side trim strips as described in the previous section, and the base is complete.

![Apply latex spackling compound to fill the joints.]

Apply latex spackling compound to fill the joints.

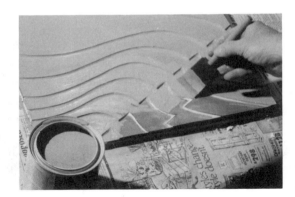

Coat with latex base paint.

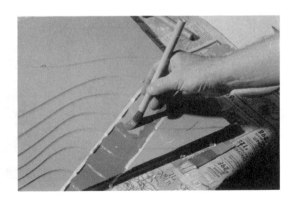

Mask and paint any paving.

## Acrylic model covers...

protect the model from dust and accidental damage during exhibition. For small models, the best and least expensive cover is a manufactured acrylic, single-layer skylight dome. These are usually available as a "replacement" unit without the skylight frame and accessories. They are typically available in standard sizes from 24" (60 cm) square up to 48" x 72" (120 cm x 180 cm).

Make sure that there is sufficient height clearance for the building model and surrounding trees. Because of this it is often necessary to select a dome size based on vertical clearance. This usually results in an oversized dome, which, in turn, requires that the model base be oversized. For this reason, it is usually desirable to select (and even purchase) the dome before beginning the model base.

## Rectilinear covers...

are commercially custom-fabricated out of clear flat acrylic in virtually any size. The glued fabrication joints are noticeably visible and fragile.

*Apply light spray texture using mouth atomizer.*

*Finished base.*

# Chapter 4:
# LANDSCAPE FEATURES

## TREES AND SHRUBS

Plant material is an important feature to a model. It should be selected with careful regard to **size, shape, texture,** and **color.**

The **size** should be selected to represent the site vegetation in its mature state (unless there is a particular reason to do otherwise). Don't underestimate the size of mature trees; the height of most mature deciduous trees is between 70 and 100' (20 to 30 m) with a spread of about two-thirds the height.

Assuming that realistic representation is desired, the profile **shape** should approximate that of tree species native to the region.

Generally speaking, the finer the **texture** of the tree the better. The foliage (especially for large scale models) should be sparse to give a light, airy feeling while providing glimpses of the building or landscape beyond. If a dense or solid material is used for large scale models, it makes the trees appear heavy and unnatural.

Because the importance of the site plants is subordinate to the building, their **colors** should be muted, natural tones (olive, tan, or brown), selected to complement the overall color scheme of the model rather that to duplicate the tree's natural colors. Avoid the "ready-made" railroad model trees at all costs; in most cases the colors of these are far to bright to be used successfully on architectural models.

Natural materials are recommended where a realistic representation of trees and shrubs is desirable.
For medium and large scale models, yarrow and Indian chief twigs are particularly well suited. When dried, they have beautiful dark brown-gray color that goes well with most model base colors.    They have a natural fan-shaped branch structure with a dome canopy of "foliage" that almost duplicates that of the American elm. Their branch structure is remarkable in that both large and small pieces can be used to simulate trees of any scale.

### Yarrow...
can be found growing naturally throughout the southeast and midwest. It is also available commercially from mail-order model supply houses (for example, Charrette, 1989) and from some florist supply houses (used for dried flower arrangements).

### Indian   Chief...
is a plant similar in shape and color to yarrow with a slightly coarser texture; it is available as a decorative garden plant from many nurseries to provide an annual "crop" of model trees.

Yarrow model trees.

Indian chief model trees.

**Reindeer moss...**
is a superb material for simulating shrubs on large and medium scale models, and small trees on small scale models. Found naturally in shaded areas of pine forests of the southeast, it is available commercially from floral suppliers, mail-order model suppliers, and model-railroad shops (as "lichen"). Undyed moss is a light gray-green color that is quite suitable for model applications.

Model-railroad "lichen" is often dyed in bright green, yellow, and even purple - colors which are too strong for architectural applications. Fortunately, the dye can be removed by soaking in water. If a darker brown color is desirable (to match yarrow, for example), use diluted sepia ink or fabric dye.

**Thistle...**
cones are abundant throughout the eastern United States and can be used to simulate large shrubs and small evergreen trees. The drab brown color goes well with most of the other natural materials listed above. Remove the "collar" leaves around the base before using.

*Reindeer moss.*

*Staining reindeer moss with sepia ink; add glycerin to maintain pliability.*

*Thistle cones for small evergreens and large shrubs.*

**Foam-sprinkled twigs...**
make good large- and medium-scale deciduous trees. Spray the top of a branched twig with spray-mount adhesive. Sprinkle with ground foam (available from model railroad shops) in muted colors selected for their compatibility with other base colors.

**Carved foam...**
can be used for small shrubs and for small-scale trees. A good source is the gray foam weatherstripping available in various thicknesses and widths (at the local hardware store or lumberyard). Color it with paint by either painting (spray or brush) or soaking/squeezing. A similar material is available in sheet as well as strip form from model mail-order suppliers (Charrette, for example).

**Printed, clear plastic trees...**
can be made by either drawing or photocopying onto a stiff, clear plastic sheet. They are most effective as bare-branch trees and have the advantage of suggesting large trees while still allowing the building to show through for presentation or photographs. They are also available commercially.

Foam for shrubs or small scale wooded areas. (Photo courtesy of Charrette, Inc.)

Printed, clear plastic trees. (Photo courtesy of Charrette, Inc.)

**Steel wool and cotton ball trees...**
are suitable for very small scale models (1" = 60' or 1:720 and smaller). Use the finest grade of steel wool, and roll lightly into balls by hand. Spray-paint to change the color (if appropriate).

**Wire and paper...**
can be used as stylized trees. Form wire trees (using fine picture wire) by making about five wraps around a round form (such as a soft-drink can) having a diameter equal to a little more than the height of the finished tree. Remove from the form, pinch one side together to form the trunk, and wrap the trunk with more wire. Reshape the top to a roughly round shape. Finally "fan" out the top wires in plan as shown in the photo. Paper trees are particularly suitable where very large stylized trees are used.

Trees created from steel wool on twigs. (Photo courtesy of IPG, Inc., Architects; 1" = 60' [1:720] model by J. Ingram and R. Hill.)

Wire trees.

Paper trees.

## SCALE FIGURES

"Populate" the model with scale figures. In addition to making the proposed design appear more humane and inviting, they provide a familiar yardstick with which to visually estimate the project's size. Figures should be of realistic size and proportions. One method of fabricating figures begins with "quilt" pins having a round head approximately 10" (25 cm) to scale; this provides the head of the figure. Usually these pins are available with white plastic heads; these can be left white for abstract figures, or colored with a marker for skin tone and hair.

To create the body, first measure 5'-8" (1.7 m) to scale on the pin for the figure height, and mark the pin with a marker. Next, cut off a length of embroidery floss in an appropriate color to represent clothing. Wrap the pin with several turns of floss, building up thickness as necessary to represent the human body (thin legs, thick torso). When the correct shape is attained, apply a little white glue to the loose end to secure it in place.

### Photo cutouts...

are particularly effective in larger scale interior models if photography is to be the primary means of presentation. Make the cutouts from magazines, or better yet from enlarged photos of the client. Make sure that the cutouts are the same scale as the model. Select subjects with conservative hair and clothing styles that are not apt to become dated.

Thread-wrapped quilt pins for scale figures.

## VEHICLES

For medium- and small-scale models, cars and trucks provide an additional scale reference. They should be a simple design without any distinguishing features that would date the model or distract attention from the project design.

If only a few vehicles are required, carve them from solid balsa. Begin with a strip that measures 2′ x 6′ (60 cm x 180 cm) to scale and a round dowel 2′ (60 cm) in diameter to scale. Cut a 17′ (5 m) length to form the lower body and an 8′ (2.5 m) length to form the roof section (11′ or 3.3 m

roof for station wagons). Sand bevels on the ends of the sections and glue them together. Cut 5′ (1.5 m) lengths of \dowel, split them with a utility knife, and glue on the bottom of the body to form the wheels. Round off the corners by sanding and paint with a neutral color.

If many vehicles are required, it may be worth the time to make a reusable mold. Begin by making (or buying) several cars. Remove the wheels and mount them on a board to create a male "plug." Next, brush on several coats of latex mold compound (available from an art supply store). This latex mold is flexible and requires a support

to maintain its shape. Cast this back support out of plaster while the original plug is still in the latex mold. When the back support is dry, remove the plug. Fill the voids with plaster to create the vehicles and allow to dry. Remove the plaster vehicles from the mold, sand off any rough edges, add split-dowel wheels, and paint.

A less elaborate, "one-off" molding process involves using modeling clay to make an impression of the plug, filling the impression void with plaster and peeling away the clay after drying.

Scale vehicles suitable for models are available commercially from mail-order

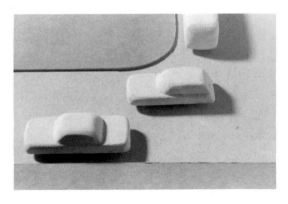

Carved balsa cars.

Toy cars painted with matte gray latex.

Molding cars: prepare the plug by gluing the wheelless cars to a base.

model suppliers at commonly used scales. Occasionally, suitable toy vehicles can be found at the right scale; often, however, their radical design makes them more suited for their intended purpose than for professional architectural applications. Inevitably, toy vehicles are brightly colored and should be repainted in a matte, neutral finish.

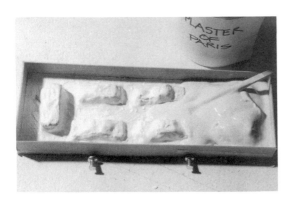

Molding cars: apply the latex mold compound.

Molding cars: rough plaster castings ready for sanding and painting.

Commercially available die cast scale model vehicles and scale figures. (Photo courtesy of Charrette, Inc.)

## WATER

### Reflecting pools...

can be rendered using glass or a glossy clear plastic (such as rigid acrylic). Paint the back of the glass prior to installation. Alternatively, illustration board may be painted and covered with a clear, glossy contact sheet of plastic (usually sold in art supply stores as "laminating" plastic).

The darkness of the color of this back-painting will determine the degree of reflection. Very dark or black back-painting creates the most dramatic "water" reflections, particularly when using a light (or white) colored model photographed against a dark sky. Uniform ripples across the entire water area can be created using a textured glass with a stippled or "hammered" finish; these give a realistic ripple effect while still providing enough reflections to make the water look "wet."

### Water streams

Localized ripples in a moving stream can be created by applying a clear glossy glue to the top of the reflecting sheet. Add spots of white tempera with a brush to create areas of turbulence (such as around rocks).

*Reflecting pond - clear plastic with a dark backing creates the most dramatic reflections. (P. Rudolf, Architect; 1/8" scale student model by M. Welling.)*

## Waterfalls

Use a sheet of clear, glossy, flexible plastic (such as report cover acetate from the local stationery store) smeared with clear glue to create a sheet waterfall.

## Fountains

For areas of water that contain a fountain, use clear, glossy laminating plastic over a colored substrate. This will permit holes to be drilled to create the fountain. Create ripples in the area of the fountain using stipples of clear glue, and let this dry. Add some stipples of white tempera with a dry brush.

Use monofilament fishing line for the spray. Begin by cutting several strands of line double the length of the height of the fountain. Group them together at one end and bind them into a brush using a wrap of transparent tape. To get the strands to curve naturally at midlength, "curl" them by drawing them between your thumb and a knife blade.

Next, drill a hole in the center of the fountain base, and insert the bound section of the "brush." Punch small holes in a circle around the center to receive the loose ends of the brush; add a dab of clear glue at each hole and insert the strand so that they appear to be "falling" naturally.

*Fountain created using monofilament fishing line.*

## ROCK  OUTCROPPINGS...

are created using plaster of paris. Add water and mix the plaster into a thick paste about the consistency of peanut butter.  If a large area of outcroppings (say, greater than 6" or 15 cm square) is to be created, slow the setting time by adding a "retarder" to the water before mixing (a few drops of white glue or vinegar). Using a flat stick, "trowel" it on over the base.  Make it deliberately uneven and lumpy.  After the plaster hardens,  carve it into rocks by first cutting deep "fissures" with a hobby knife and then slicing off flat areas to simulate the angular faceted shapes of natural outcropping.

After the plaster dries (preferably overnight), prewet the plaster with a wash of clear water, then add a wash of dark gray watercolor over the stone;  the wash will collect in the cracks to make the stone darkest there resulting in a very natural effect.

While it is possible to further enhance the rocks using model-railroad scenery techniques (for example, simulating lichen and moss by sparsely sifting a dry mixture of plaster powder and powdered watercolor over the rewetted rocks; see Warren, 1975; also McClanahan, 1976), such superrealism tends to distract attention from the main subject - the building.

Rock outcropping: mask the base and apply thick plaster mixture.

Rock outcropping:  carve with knife and color with watercolor.

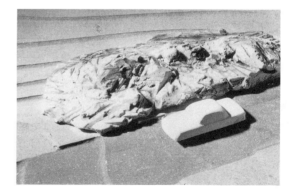

Finished rock outcropping.

# Chapter 5:
# SMALL-SCALE BUILDINGS

### SCALE

Large site models are typically built at scales of 1" - 40' (1:480) and smaller. This scale range is selected where there are large site features that must be represented (including those such as roads, topography, wooded and planted areas, adjacent buildings, etc.). Consequently, the small scale of the proposed building(s) necessitates showing only its overall form, with no facade details. Site models with large buildings are usually built at scales between 1" - 30' (1:360) and 3/32" - 1'-0" (1:128). This scale range permits showing all of the major fenestration and exterior facade features and colors, as well as small areas of the surrounding landscape. However, at this scale, it is both difficult and undesirable to show facade details such as mullions, masonry coursing, joints, textures, trim, etc.

### Illustration board...

is suited for building hollow models of buildings in this scale range. For low- and medium-rise flat-roofed buildings, it is usually not necessary to build a "floor" of the building model. Build only the walls and roof. Begin by laying out the roof plan of the building on illustration board. Reduce the perimeter dimensions by the thickness of the board on all sides. Lay out and render the walls (windows are usually drawn). Cut out the walls and roof(s), and glue the walls around the roof.

1" - 100' (1:1200) water front development master plan site model (William Turnbull Associates, Architects).

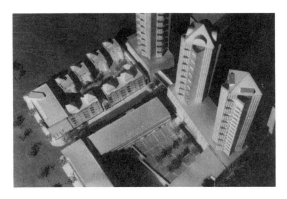

1" - 30' (1:360) student project model (by A. Agarwal, B. Babajide, B. Christianson, S. Hoon, S. Li, S. Olmedo, J. Roberts, and L. Yan.)

Urban development project white Strathmore illustration board model. (KZF Inc., Architects; 3/8" scale [1:32] model by P. Moore.)

## Photocopied facades

If elevation drawings are available, the facades can be photocopied to greatly reduce model construction time. Photocopy the elevations onto the heaviest available "cover" paper (about the thickness of an index card). The scale can be changed by using photocopiers having enlarging-reducing capabilities. Glue the facades around the roof. Because of the difficulty in obtaining precisely scaled enlargements (photocopiers usually enlarge or reduce in whole percentage amounts), lay out the roof based on measurements directly from the photocopies.

It is possible to use create depth in the facades by taking advantage of the photocopier's capability to make exact duplicate copies on heavy card stock quickly and at low cost. Begin with a hollow illustration-board box (stiffer for rigidity) for the core of the building. Next apply a photocopy of the facade to the surface. Next, cut out all window openings from a second facade photocopy. Glue some spacer strips of white illustration board around the window openings on the back of the photocopy and glue onto the building model. The spacer strips add depth to the facade especially when viewed (or photographed) with a sharp, oblique light source.

Repeat the process as necessary to build up the important projections on the building facade. Different colored card stock can be used for the photocopies to increase contrast between building materials. This technique is especially effective in modeling ornate traditional buildings. Hardwoods should be shaped with a power table saw, provided the shapes are simple enough. In general, power tools such as a table saw take time to set up and are most suitable where a large number of repetitive elements must be fabricated.

Housing prototypes. (Design and 1" = 20' [1:240] model by Gerardo Brown-Manrique, Architect.)

Large building model (layered facades were made using elevations photocopied onto 60 lb white "cover" paper).

## Foam board...

which is available in thicknesses from 3/16" to 1/2" (5 mm to 13 mm), can be used to quickly create small building mass models, provided that the thickness of the board corresponds to the scaled story height of the model (for example, using 1/4" or 6 mm foam board to represent 10' or 3 m stories on a 1" = 40' or 1:480 site model).

Without painting and covering exposed foam edges, this material is suited only for preliminary study models. Other material (such as heavy white paper) must be used to create nonflat roof shapes.

## Carved foam

A hot-wire cutter can be used to quickly shape blocks of polystyrene foam for mass and site models. The thin hot wire makes a smooth cut even through thick blocks of foam. Because the fumes from the melting polystyrene are both obnoxious and toxic, use these cutters only in a well-vented area.

## Wood...

can be used to create simple building forms for small-scale site models. It is an attractive choice if the building shape is simple and the size corresponds to available wood stock dimensions. Balsa can be easily cut to length using a fine-toothed saw, sanded, and painted. Staining is not recommended for this and other soft woods because the porous end grain absorbs more stain and finishes darker than the sides and top. Hardwoods (such as walnut, basswood, etc.) can be used. They can be shaped with a power table saw, provided the shapes are simple enough and a large number of repetitive elements must be created.

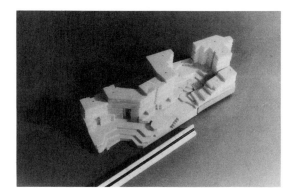

Foam board design model (William Turnbull Associates / KZF, Inc., Architects; 1" = 40' [1:480] model by J. Koster).

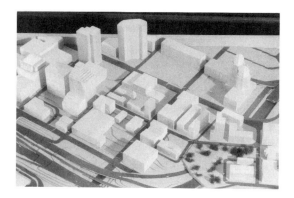

1" = 100' (1:1200) urban site model with wood existing buildings (William Turnbull Associates, Architects).

## Clay

Although modeling clay is traditionally used only for design models (because of the ease with which changes in building massing can be made), it is used by some designers for small-scale presentation models.  It is well-suited for this application where the scale is very small, or the landforms of the site are sculpted to become an integral part of the design composition. Professional quality clay is available in large "bricks" in green-gray and putty colors.

1" = 100' (1:1200) clay mass buildings of riverfront development master plan (William Turnbull Associates, Architects).

# Chapter 6:
# MEDIUM-SCALE BUILDINGS

Models of this scale are large enough to show most of the design decisions that are made during the design development phase, while omitting minor construction details without the model appearing unfinished. They are easily constructed out of white, single-layer sheet material that is rendered with drawing techniques to show textures and minor surface configurations.

## Interior visibility

The amount of the interior that will be visible or available for viewing will have a major effect on the complexity of the model and will affect the method of construction. Completely revealing the interior can easily double the construction time.

In general, a scale appropriate for an exterior model is too small to show anything except major interior partitions and the largest furnishings. These interior features can be more efficiently represented in a drawing. Therefore, combination exterior-interior models are recommended only for small buildings with a small site where a comparatively large scale is selected.

If the interior is to be shown on two-story buildings, it is recommended that the roof and upper floor (and interior partitions) be removable, with all exterior walls remaining fixed. This combination eliminates the necessity for assembly joints on the exterior walls, which are difficult to conceal.

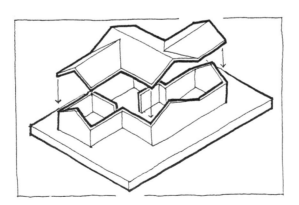

*Single story - removable roof; interior partitions are visible.*

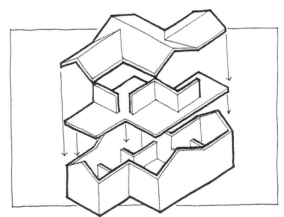

*Two-story - roof and upper floor/interior partitions are removable to reveal first floor partitions; single-layer wall construction.*

## Wall thickness

There is a speed-accuracy tradeoff in the representation of wall thickness. Single-layer exterior walls require much less time to construct and should be used in all locations where

- The interior will not be shown.

- Wall thickness is not an important design consideration.

- Windows are not substantially recessed.

Use sandwich or "stud" wall construction only where the interior is to be shown and the thickness is a major design consideration (i.e., thick, "poche" walls

where both surfaces are not parallel), or where the deep reveals around windows are of major design importance in the appearance of the facade.

## "On" or "in" the base?

For level sites, simply construct the model to rest on the base (unless underground areas are to be visible).

For sloped sites, where the terrain slopes at the building perimeter, the building-ground intersection is more complex. It is usually easier to "trim the contours to fit around the model" (rather than vice versa). Increase the height of the building model accordingly by adding the distance from the subbase up to the grade surface.

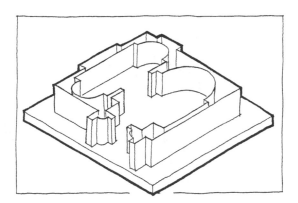

Multilayer wall construction for "poche" wall: at 1/8" scale (1:96) single-ply Strathmore is shaped to conform to the perimeter of each room separately.

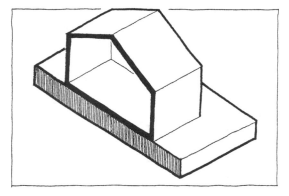

Model "on" the base (building rests on level base).

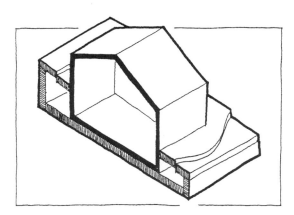

Model "in" the base (sloped base is cut to receive building).

## Sheet material selection

In general, use a high-quality white paper or board (such as cold-pressed Strathmore board in a thickness from one to five layers) that can be rendered using various "drawing" techniques (pencil, pen, marker, pastel, watercolor, etc.) instead of commercially prepared boards.   At this scale, almost any building material can be realistically simulated using these techniques which are quick, learnable, inexpensive, and above all always available and convenient.

The rationale behind this strategy has less to do with material cost savings than with the difficulty of anticipating and purchasing all of the needed colors and textures in advance. Invariably, searching for a small sheet of illustration board in just the right color can be a time-consuming task - more so than rendering a white board or paper using drawing materials. It minimizes the necessity for stockpiling a large supply of different colored illustration boards and special surface materials.

For models with single-layer surfaces, use five-ply cold-pressed 100% rag board (for example, Strathmore ).   It is easy to lay out on a drafting board, and has an excellent medium-tooth surface that takes a variety of useful rendering mediums: pencil, ink, marker, paint, colored pencil, pastel.   A particularly valuable quality of this board is its white core, which allows edges to be colored to match the surface before gluing (making the exposed edges at corners almost invisible).   It is stiff enough to span up to 4" with no additional support, and cuts easily with a utility knife, producing sharp, square edges. Finally, it glues easily with white glue and is available at most art supply stores at moderate cost.

For thicker walls, use multiple layers of five-ply board, or one- or two-ply paper laminated over a core such as foam board (the semiglossy surface of foam board makes marker and watercolor apply unevenly, resulting in a streaked appearance).    If foam board is used, it is necessary to cover the exposed foam edges.    This can be done in several ways, all of which are somewhat tedious: (1) paper glued on (cut into strips, glue using white glue), (2) pressure-sensitive paper correction tape (3/16" width, available at office supply stores), or  (3) Zip-a-Line tape (pressure-sensitive, available in various bright colors and widths at art supply stores).

## Construction  sequence

In general, the following sequence of steps (which are subsequently described in detail) is recommended for constructing medium-scale exterior models:

1.  Lay out all major parts of the model (footprint, floors, exterior walls, roof) lightly in pencil by drafting onto a sheet of white illustration board.

2.  Render the exposed model surfaces, applying all coloring (marker, etc.) to the drafted board.

3.  Cut all pieces using a straightedge and utility knife.

4.  Color all exposed edges to match the adjacent surface.

5.  Assemble and glue the pieces together (ideally, no cutting or coloring after gluing).

6.  Scribe the outline of the building onto the model base, cut out the opening to receive the model, and glue the model into (onto) the base.

7.  Add exterior building accessories.

# 1. LAYOUT

Lay out the outline footprint of the building less the perimeter wall material thickness on five-ply board (this will be the bottom of the building model, and all of the perimeter walls will be applied around this footprint).

## Interior floors and partitions layout

If the interior is to be visible (either through removable roof or large glass areas), lay out each floor plan, lightly showing the location of the interior partitions in pencil.

Take special care to lay out each floor accurately. A little extra care here will have a major effect on the overall precision and craftsmanship of the model.

## Facade layout

Lay out all of the facades in pencil, taking width measurements directly from the footprint and systematically allowing for the board thicknesses in laying out these facades:

- Lay out all east and west facades full width.

- Lay out all north and south facades full width less the thickness of the east and west wall surfaces.

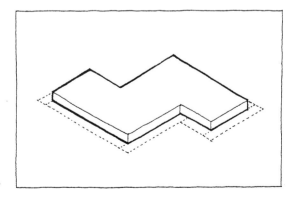

Lay out footprint less perimeter wall thickness.

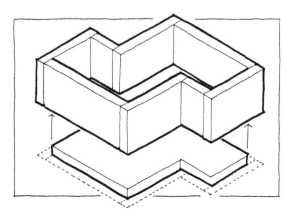

Systematically allow for board thicknesses when laying out facades.

## Roof layout
**Flat roofs** with parapet are constructed similar to floors so that the walls extend above the roof. For overhangs, apply a fascia strip to increase the apparent thickness of the roof structure. Because the "soffit" is not usually visible, it is not necessary to actually build up the roof thickness.

For a **gable roof**, determine the sloped dimensions by measuring directly from the end facade, and make allowances for the type of ridge joint to be used.

For a **hip roof**, accurate sections through the roof showing the slope and true length along the slope are required in order to construct the segments.

**Conical roofs** are formed using heavy paper cut in a pieshape and bent into a cone. Measure along the slope on a vertical section through the center of the cone to determine the radius of the pieshape. Draw a circle on the paper using this radius. The angle (in degrees) of the pieshape is equal to the cosine of the roof slope angle x 360°. Add about 3/16" (5 mm) for overlap.

Because **domes** are curved in two directions, they cannot be formed out of flat material. If possible, adapt ready-made objects, such as a toy ball or polystyrene foam sphere (Christmas tree ornament or florist materials). Small elements can be formed from children's hobby clay, which hardens in an oven. Another alternative for domes (and other freeform shapes) is to cast a solid block of plaster and use a wood rasp and sandpaper for shaping. It is possible to gravity-form a dome from a thin sheet of acrylic slowly heated in an oven. Cut a round hole the diameter of the base of the dome in a piece of plywood. Staple sheet acrylic (about 0.05" or 1 mm thick) around the edge of the hole. Support the plywood in the oven so that there is clearance below for the dome to sag into as it is heated.

Measure the true dimensions of the hip roof segments directly from the sections.

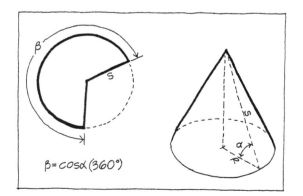

$$\beta = \cos\alpha\,(360°)$$

Construction of conical roof.

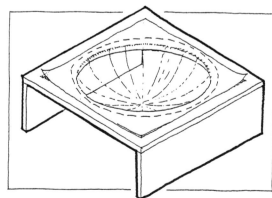

Heat-forming an acrylic dome.

**Tension structures** (such as tents) can be modeled easily using stretch fabrics such as T-shirt material, nylon hose, and double-knits. The natural curvatures that are created when these fabrics are stretched over vertical supports provide the designer with insights into the behavior and appropriate forms of tension structures. In addition the technique is simple, finished in appearance, and difficult to achieve in other ways.

Commercially available acrylic domes. (Photograph courtesy of Charrette, Inc.)

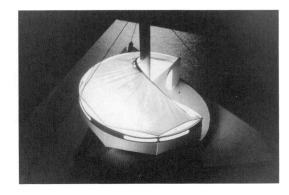

Tension fabric roof created by stretching T-shirt fabric. (Model by S. Johnston.)

## 2.  RENDERING  SURFACES

For convenience and uniformity of application, color and/or texture all surfaces before cutting.  See Chapter 2 for a comparison of the most useful mediums for rendering model surfaces.

In rendering materials on model surfaces, make sure that the amount of detail is appropriate to the scale (and purpose) of the model.  For example, at large scales (for example, 3/8" or 1:32 and larger) it is appropriate to show each individual brick defined with both vertical and horizontal joints.  At 1/8" - 1'-0" (1:96), this amount of detail begins to appear somewhat fussy, distracting attention from other more important features of the model.  Simply ruling the horizontal joints (to give a feeling of texture to the surface) is more appropriate.  At 1/20" (1:240) scale, no joints should be shown at all.

Scale accuracy is very important in rendering materials.  Nothing destroys the illusion of scale quicker than, for example, drawing brick courses 4" (10 cm) wide.  These are interpreted visually as the familiar 2 $^2$/3" (67 mm) spacing, and the building appears to be a smaller building at a larger model scale.  Other familiar objects, such as scale figures and vehicles, must be the correct size for the same reasons.

Color is also important in scale modeling.  If colors on the model are made to exactly match their full-scale counterpart, they will appear too intense and often incompatible with one another.  This is especially true for landscape materials on exterior models at smaller scales.  In general, medium colors (paints, pastels, pencils, etc.) are too intense for direct use on architectural model applications and should be grayed slightly. Do this by the addition of the complementary color (add a touch of red, for example, to green to get olive color). A collection of techniques for rendering various building materials in appropriate modeling scales is presented in Appendix A.

Case study exterior model of private residence. (Briner/Strain Architects; 1/8" scale [1:96] model by author.)

After drafting detail on white five-ply illustration board, apply color using broad marker and straightedge.

Wood siding colored with marker over inked siding and window frames.

## Windows and glass

Windows are important design features of a building and may be represented in a variety of ways.

For small- and medium-scale exterior models, where the interior is not to be revealed, and window size is small, the simplest method of making them opaque may be the most appropriate.   Solid black is recommended because interiors are very dark in comparison with the exterior.   In addition, the strong contrast between black and the surrounding wall colors abstractly represents the solid-void contrast inherent in windows.   Blue (for sky reflections) is not recommended because

sky reflections are virtually never visible from normal model viewing angles.

The next stage of window realism is to cut out empty voids on exterior models. If appropriate, color the edge of the cutout.  If the windows are comparatively small, the interior is still very dark and need not be finished.

As the model scale or window size becomes larger and as glass becomes a dominant design element, reflections become more important. Once the windows are cut out, it becomes a simple procedure to add real reflections by applying an oversized piece of clear plastic applied to the back of the cutout.

For all but the smallest windows, it is essential that the plastic be rigid to prevent distortions in the reflections. These distorted reflections destroy the illusion of reality; better to omit the plastic entirely than to use a flexible material.

As glass areas become very large and wrap around corners, opaque materials (such as mullions) become less significant and reflections become essential in defining the shape of the building enclosure.   Rigid plastic is not only necessary to prevent reflection distortion, but it also becomes a necessary structural element of the model.   In a predominantly glass building, it is often more efficient to

Opaque black windows. (Barcus, Moore, Zwirn, Architects; 1/8" scale [1:96] model by G. Bennett.)

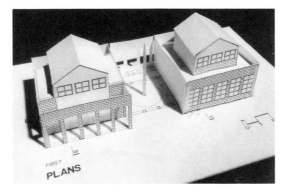

Opaque white windows. (Design and 1:120 model by Gerardo Brown-Manrique, Architect.)

build the walls out of clear acrylic sheet and apply strips to represent columns and mullions.  Make the corners of the acrylic using butt joints and "superglue"; cover the joint with Zip-a-line tape.

These applied strips may be balsa (or basswood) or illustration board, all colored with marker prior to application.  For very thin mullions, use Zip-a-line tape, which is available in black, white (which can be stained with marker prior to application), silver, and a variety of bright colors.  This versatile "tape" is pressure-sensitive and is available in various widths from $3/8$" to $1/64$" (10 mm to 0.4 mm) at artist supply stores.

Alternatively, mullions can be "drawn" on with ink (or a hobby enamel suitable for plastics) using a ruling pen.  Prepare the plastic by rubbing with "pounce" powder; this will prevent the ink from "beading up" (available from drafting suppliers; intended for preparing drafting cloth and Mylar for inking).

Curved glass (for example, greenhouses) is made of flexible clear plastic bent over curved end supports. Apply any mullions using Zip-a-line prior to installing the plastic.

Closely spaced mullions represent large areas of glass.  (Student model by A. Sorkin and M. Turin.)

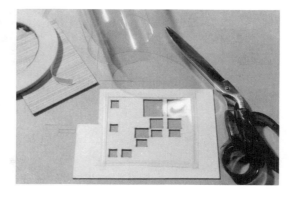

Clear plastic applied to back of cutout.

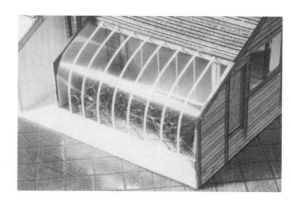

Greenhouse created using Zip-a-line on clear "report cover" acetate bent over curved illustration form on each end.

## 3.  CUTTING  COMPONENTS

Once the facades have been rendered, cut out the components using a straightedge and matte knife.

Tips for quick and accurate cutting:

- Put a protective cutting surface under the material to be cut.

- Put the point of the knife at the end of the cut line.

- Slide the straightedge against the knife point, and pivot the other end of the straightedge around to the cut line. (This is much easier than trying to simultaneously align both ends.)

- Reposition the knife to the beginning of the cut line.

- Holding the straightedge down firmly, draw the knife the full length of the cut using moderate to light pressure.

- Use two cuts on all but the thinnest board; the heavy pressure necessary for a reliable single cut makes the knife blade flex and wander off from the straightedge.

- Make sure that all cuts go completely through the board; if necessary, cut again. Avoid the temptation, especially on inside corner cuts, to tear the piece out rather than recutting those few remaining fibers holding the corner together.

Large acrylic windows.

Cut out facades using straightedge.

## 4. COLORING CUT EDGES

Once all pieces are cut, color all of the exposed white edges of the pieces. It is important to do this before gluing; once glue is applied, the "surface" changes dramatically and will not match surrounding areas. For example, marker will not "take" at all over dried glue resulting in white gaps in the coloring.

If marker is used, because the exposed endgrain of the board is more absorbent than the surface, the edge will be slightly darker if the same color marker is used as for the surface. To compensate, use a lighter shade of the same color.

Color the edges using marker after cutting, but before gluing.

## 5.   COMPONENT   ASSEMBLY

### Test   fitting
Always test-fit important pieces before gluing to ensure size and shape fit and to visualize which surfaces or edges should receive glue application.

### Gluing...
is an important and underrated skill in modelbuilding.   The objective, of course, is to make strong joints without unsightly excess glue.

Apply glue very sparingly using the finger to "wipe" a fine line of glue onto the edge of the component by dragging the finger slowly over the corner edge. Wait a few seconds to let the glue begin to air-dry.   Then touch the two pieces together where they are joined, and slide the pieces back and forth to assure good contact and to spread out the glue over the entire joint.   Hold the pieces in place for a few seconds and release and let dry.   Wipe off any excess glue using the fingers.

### Alignment
Take special care to ensure that the major walls and "footprint" are aligned true and perpendicular. Check alignment frequently using drafting triangles.
Install hidden vertical "corner brackets" to help maintain perpendicular alignment between the walls and footprint.

*Assemble the walls around the floors.*

## Intermediate floors...

(if required) are installed after the first two major perpendicular walls are installed. Use spacers to maintain floor-to-floor heights.

## Install roof...

after all walls and interior components are in place. If the roof is to be permanently fixed, install hidden corner braces near the top of the walls to maintain the upper wall shape prior to gluing the roof into place. If the roof is to be removable, glue some small, concealed, cardboard "stops" on the bottom of the roof surface to help align the roof on the walls while providing some lateral support to the upper wall when the roof is in place.

*Detail of roof ridge (single-ply paper colored with marker; crease with stylus and cut with knife).*

*Building model after roofs are installed.*

## 6. INSTALLING THE BUILDING

Scribe the outline of the building model onto the base by tracing around the bottom with a sharp instrument, such as a straight pin taped to the side of a holder (such as a piece of dowel), or a pencil.

Cut along the building outline to create a hole in the base to receive the building.  Cut the contours using a sharp utility knife. If the slope of the site is steep, and the contours are stepped, then scribe and cut the top few contours.  Repeat as necessary to assure an accurate fit.

Test-fit the model to assure a good fit. Check that doorsills line up with correct grade heights.  Finally, glue the building model permanently into place by applying glue to the sides of the opening (never on the building model), so that the glue remains hidden as the model is slid into place.

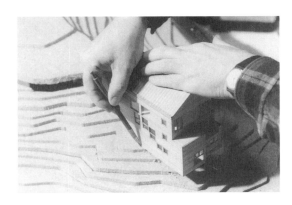

*Tracing around the model.*

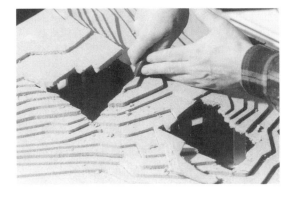

*Cut the building opening in the base.*

## 7.  BUILDING ACCESSORIES

**Railings  and  balusters...**
are tedious to build up using stick materials such as balsa or basswood. It is difficult to maintain alignment and spacing while working with the extremely thin materials necessary to maintain scale.  To facilitate this, either lay out the spacing of the components on a sheet of paper and cut or assemble the balsa directly on this layout.  Spacer blocks or strips can be used to ensure uniform and repetitive alignment.  Folded masking tape can be used to temporarily hold the members in place prior to gluing.

An efficient alternative is to form the railing area out of a sheet of clear, thin acrylic and apply Zip-a-line tape to represent the railing and ballusters. The acrylic becomes virtually invisible (in comparison with all of the visual prominence of the tape) and can be creased for corners.

*Balsa railings: use double sided tape over pencil layout to hold pieces temporarily in place for gluing.*

*Acrylic railings: use pencil layout below clear acrylic to guide positioning of Zip-a-line. Trim acrylic and bend at corners prior to installation.*

**Covered  walks  and  canopies...**
are usually constructed and added after the building model is permanently installed in (or on) the base.  While the main part of the building model is a comparatively rigid assembly, these "add-ons" are frequently  fragile appendages that are best constructed "in place."

## Stairs...

are inherently tedious due to their repetitive geometry and the relatively small size of the individual treads. At small scales (1" = 20' [1:240] and smaller), stairs can be simulated with a sloped piece of illustration board, with lines drafted to represent the nosing of each tread. However, at larger scales, individual treads should be constructed for finished presentation models. These individual treads adds a level of detail that contributes substantially to the realism of the model.

Construct the stair tread section using balsa strips having a thickness equal to the riser height of the stair (6" [15 cm] for exterior stairs, 7" [17 cm] to 8" [20 cm] for interior stairs). For all but the simplest stairs, a jig should be used to hold the individual treads in proper spacing and alignment.

Glue each tread to the previous one and finally reinforce with a bead of glue along the length of the section (for even greater strength, add a backing of a strip of illustration board). Paint after glue is dry. If several sections of stair are required, make a single wide section and cut into narrower strips.

## Walks and paved areas...

If the paving follows the site contours, lay out and paint the paving directly on the contours prior to installing the building model. If necessary, transfer the layout of the paving from the site plan. Either mask out paving area before painting using a low-tack tape to prevent lifting the paint below (for example, drafting tape) or outline the area using a ruling pen...or directly with a brush, if you have a steady hand. Paint the area a neutral and slightly contrasting color. If the paving area is level (such as a patio), build up the area using illustration board. Render the materials in the same manner as other building materials (see Appendix A).

*Stair jig for temporary support of treads is made of illustration board. Treads seen from "below" positioned on jig and glue applied to back.*

*Stair installation.*

*Mask and paint paving.*

## LANDSCAPE   ACCESSORIES

Add trees, vehicles, and scale figures
(see Chapter 4) and the model is
complete.

Paved patio area with stone retaining
wall. Plants are natural reindeer moss
(lichen).

Completed case study model - from the
northwest. (Private residence,
Briner/Strain Architects; 1/8" scale
[1:96] model by the author.)

From the southwest.

# Chapter 7:
# INTERIOR MODELS

Interior models can be classified as detailed room models and furniture layout models.

## DETAILED ROOM MODELS...

are usually for design study or client presentation of interior design features including room configuration, furniture layout and selection, finishes (wall, floor, and ceiling), equipment, and accessories. In order to show the significant details (which are smaller in physical size than exterior details of comparable importance) the scale should be larger:  at least 3/8" = 1-0". The following is a case study of the construction of a model of a residence. See design drawings in Appendix D.

## Layout

Begin by laying out the floor plan in pencil on a piece of white cold-pressed five-ply 100% rag illustration board.  In most cases, it is simpler to plan the model so that the floor extends under the walls (rather that having the walls built around the outside of the floor). The exception would be where more than one floor level must be shown.

Prototype commercial shop interior. (Photo courtesy of Space Design International; 1/4" scale [1:48] model by G. Humphrey.)

Hotel room interior.  (3/4" scale [1:16] student project by S.  Johnston.)

Case study residence interior. (Briner/Strain Architects; 3/8" scale [1:32] model by author.)

## Rendering the floor

Next, render the flooring materials. In this example, most of the flooring is oak planks of random length. Using parallel bar and triangle, draft the joints of the flooring using a very sharp 2H pencil. Make the lines dark since their contrast will be reduced by the subsequent overlay of marker color.

To color the flooring, first run a uniform "wash" of light tan marker. Use the widest flat of the marker against the triangle (protect the edge with a layer of masking tape). For this first wash try not to overlap (or leave any gaps) - the objective is a uniform color with no streaks.

Go back and overlay with the same color to create dark stripes the width of the planks using the thinner width of the same broad marker tip. These should be of random length. With the pencil, add the end joints of the planking at all of the ends of the dark planks and at other random locations.

Because reflections become very important at this scale, add a clear, semigloss finish over all of the wood planking by adding a layer of pressure-sensitive clear vinyl contact sheet. Cut the sheet oversize and rough to shape; strip off the backing paper and lay it lightly over the flooring area; rub lightly from the center out toward the perimeter, removing air bubbles. Prick

the vinyl with a pin or knifepoint to work out any trapped air bubbles.

Using a utility knife and straightedge, trim exactly to the line of exposure of the flooring and remove the excess vinyl. In particular, do not let excess vinyl extend under wall locations because of the difficulty in later gluing walls to the vinyl. Burnish the vinyl using a straightedge (such as a drafting triangle).

In this example, the kitchen area flooring is handmade ceramic tile. Lay out the joints in pencil, dark enough to be seen after the application of marker. Apply a uniform wash of

Wood flooring - cover flooring with semigloss, pressure-sensitive vinyl contact sheet.

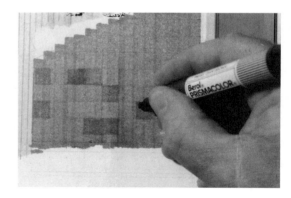

Ceramic tile - apply marker basecoat and then darken random tiles with a second coat of marker.

Wood flooring - render the wood flooring with marker color on five-ply illustration board; define joints with 2H pencil.

marker using a straightedge. Using the same marker, apply a second coat to darken random tiles. Draw the grout joints between tiles using a ruling pen and straightedge to apply tan tempera.

To give the tile its characteristic high gloss, apply clear, high-gloss pressure-sensitive laminating sheets in the same manner as above. Finally, for large scales, score the grout lines with a stylus (or empty ball-point pen). This will break up the reflections of the large area into individual tiles to create a very realistic appearance.

## Interior partitions

Once the floor is completed, construct and install major interior partitions and fixed objects. In this example, a large stone room divider is a dominant interior design feature. It consists of a fireplace, wood storage, sitting bench with upholstered cushion, and bookshelves.

Lay out the divider, and draw the outlines of the random stones. To make the stones realistic, draw them so that they will wrap continuously around the corners when the structure is assembled. This requires some measuring so that the joints will line up, but it is important if the stone is to not look like

a thin veneer applied separately to each face. Color all of the stones with marker prior to cutting and assembly (remember that marker will not "take" over dried glue).

For the logs, first stain (with marker) and then cut hardwood dowels with a utility knife. The upholstered cushion is cut from a 3/16" (5 mm) piece of foam board that is edge-wrapped with paper, and painted with tempera. The bookshelves are strips of white illustration board colored with marker. The books are also white illustration board striped with color and glued onto the shelves.

Line grout joints using the ruling pen and tempera.

Cover the rendered tiles with laminating plastic.

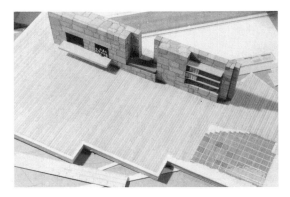

Glue the stone divider onto the floor.

The island counter is constructed of white illustration board, with the curved end formed using matching white paper bent over curved illustration board forms.  Joints are ink ruled, and the "wood" edge trim is a separate strip of thin white illustration board, stained with marker before gluing.

The cooking range is made of white illustration board on the sides and front, and foil-covered illustration board on the top with detailed drafted on in black ink.  The stainless steel backsplash and hood are foil-faced illustration board.

The closet door and siding are marker-colored and overdrawn with black ink to show joints and shadows. In order to allow for camera access when photographing the model interior, the kitchen island, closet, stove, and end wall are all assembled as a removable unit.

The counters and cabinets are made of white illustration board with drafted ink joints, covered with semigloss plastic to increase reflections. These, together with the refrigerator, are preassembled as a single wall unit.

### Furniture

Construct and install most furniture before installing the exterior walls (once the walls are in place, it is difficult to place and adjust furniture).

It is very difficult to accurately model most commercial furniture designs.  For that reason, if possible, use "generic" furniture of simple design that is easy to fabricate and gives the room scale and a furnished look without committing the designer to a specific furniture type at the time of the model construction.

It is very important that the scale of the furniture be correct.  Because the standard size of furniture is so familiar

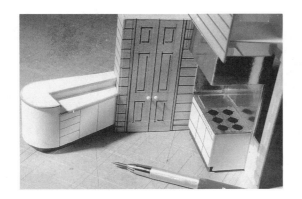

*Counter-closet-stove-end wall assembly.*

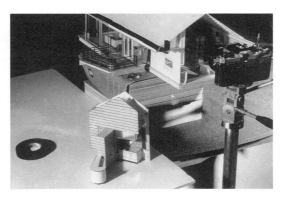

*Build the end wall, island, stove, and closet as a removable unit for camera access.*

to most people, using oversized or undersized model furniture will distort the apparent size of the room. While at first this may seem to be a useful deception (making the room seem larger or more intimate than it actually is) to help the designer "sell" the design to the client, in the end it usually results in client dissatisfaction: "The room seems a lot smaller than it did in the model."

Simple club chairs and sofas are compatible with most interior styles and can be easily modeled using foam board. To create a more finished appearance, the foam edge may be sealed either by covering with paper or by wiping with latex spackling compound. Paint with tempera.

Less bulky furniture, such as dining room table and chairs, can be easily constructed using five-ply illustration board stained with marker before assembly. By comparison, designs which use "sticks" for legs are unusually tedious because of the difficulty of properly aligning four legs. The dining set shown below took about 20 minutes total to construct (all of the parts were laid out together and cut together for considerable time savings); by contrast, a comparably detailed set with stick legs would take several hours to construct.

See Appendix B for construction drawings for a variety of generic furniture types suitable for model construction.

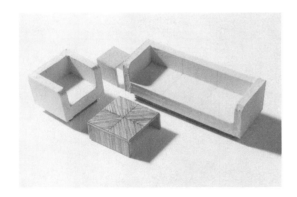

3/8" scale (1:32) club chair and sofa made of foam board, and painted with tempera.

3/8" scale (1:32) dining set made of marker-stained Strathmore board.

### Plants...

are important accessories in most interiors. They are easily represented in the model using reindeer moss (lichen). A variety of "found" plastic caps, etc., can be used for containers.

### Rugs and carpet...

are easily simulated using paper. Velour paper looks like fine velvet and can be used to simulate a deep plush carpet. Color the velour with pastel powder applied with a cotton ball. Use plain bond paper (colored with pastels or mouth atomizer) for thinner, commercial grade carpets. Patterned rugs can be drawn on bond paper with either colored pencils or marker (watch the bleeding into adjacent areas with marker; it's difficult to control).

### Draperies...

should be made of bond paper colored with marker (or colored charcoal paper). Fold the paper to simulate pleats; be careful that the folds look natural the way that gravity would make the real fabric drape naturally. For translucent fabrics, use either white tracing paper or photographic lens cleaning tissue. Do not use actual fabric for the model material. Virtually all fabrics are visually too coarse and stiff to represent the natural draping of full-scale fabrics.

House plant (reindeer moss) in planter (painted half of film canister).

Handwoven rug made of marker colored bond paper; edge fringe is drawn with pencil.

Lay out, draft, color, and cut perimeter walls.

### Perimeter walls

Once the furniture is installed, lay out the exterior walls on white five-ply illustration board. Draft the joints and shadow lines using ink, and color using an appropriate medium (in this example, marker is appropriate for coloring the natural-finish redwood paneling and trim). Cut out the parts using a utility knife and straightedge, and color the exposed edges with marker. Apply clear, rigid plastic to the backs of openings for glazing. Use small pieces of double-sided tape to add thin illustration board mullions on the glazing plastic.

### Exposed roof trusses

Begin by prestaining all balsa to be used for the trusses with marker pens before cutting. Draft the layout of the truss onto a scrap of illustration board and glue on small blocks ("stops") to create a simple jig. Cut out the basic pieces for one truss and use these as cutting templates to precut all of the pieces for all of the remaining trusses. Glue the pieces together within the jig to form identical trusses.

### Ceiling

Give the ceiling the same care as the other more visible surfaces in the model. Remember, in eye-level photographs, the ceiling will be more visible than the floor (which is usually obscured by furniture).

In the example design, the ceiling exposes the bottom edge of the 2x10 (2 cm x 20 cm) wood roof joists, with the space between joists filled with white plaster. The visual effect of this exposed joist construction is a white ceiling with wood strips (24" [60 cm] o.c.) running the length of the roof and perpendicular to the trusses.

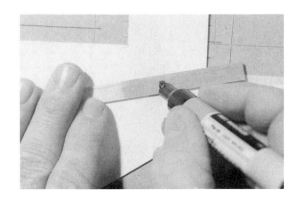

Before cutting, prestain all balsa truss members using marker.

Build a simple perimeter jig to maintain the size and shape of the trusses.

Ceiling panels with exposed joist bottoms - prestained square balsa strips applied to white Strathmore board.

The model is constructed the way the design appears. White five-ply illustration board is used for the plaster ceiling and balsa strips (prestained with marker) are glued onto the illustration board.

Electric lighting...

may be added to the interior to suggest the **presence** of artificial illumination on the interior space. In practice, it is not possible at model scale to accurately simulate the distribution patterns and intensity of full size fixtures. Furthermore, model lighting components are comparatively dim and "warm" in color; thus, they are unsatisfactory as the sole source of illumination for photographing the model interior. If windows and skylights are included in the design, it is preferable to supplement the interior model lighting fixtures with "daylight" illumination from exterior studio lights.

While finished 1" scale (1:12) miniature lamp fixtures are available through hobby shops, their high level of detail and typically traditional design make them unsuitable for most professional design applications. However, the wiring systems and bulbs available for the miniature hobby market are well suited for the present purpose.

"Tapewire" is applied like adhesive tape. It consists of two solid copper strips imbedded in the adhesive side of tape. By peeling off the paper backing, the tapewire is applied directly to the back surfaces of model walls, floor, or ceiling wherever lighting is required.

Interior of finished case study model (from the west).

Interior model with electric lighting. (Model by E. Cobb, A. Green, E. Koch, and J. Wagner; photo courtesy of M. Millet.)

For a small number of lights that are only to be used for short periods, it is simplest to use a 12 volt transistor battery as the power source. For larger or more prolonged applications, a small transformer is recommended to allow the 12V bulbs to be used with 110V AC household current. Battery and transformer kits are available.

A wide variety of miniature incandescent bulbs are available, most with integral wires to facilitate installation.

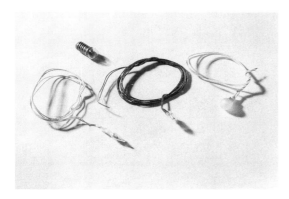

"Grain-of-wheat," grain-of-rice," frosted "pea," and screw-in miniature bulbs.

## FURNITURE LAYOUT MODELS

Interior models at a scale of 1/8" to 1/4" = 1'-0" (1:48) are too small to easily show the necessary detail of interior features and furniture, and they are too small to permit eye-level photographs (due to the limited depth of focus inherent with close focusing distances. They are, however, excellent for studying furniture layouts. The size is sufficiently large to allow visualization of the space when it is occupied, yet small enough to allow use of abstract furniture forms.

The basic structure of the model is the same as described above for larger models. However, the smaller physical size of the model often allows five-ply white illustration board to be used without fear of warping. At this scale, construct the model with fixed walls and a removable ceiling. Although textures and colors can be added, these design models are more typically left white or neutral gray.

The basic furniture forms should be very abstract, and thus easy to represent in model form. Five-ply white illustration board is an excellent material for the furniture. However, because the furniture is so light in weight, it is easily jarred out of place. Use small strips of double-sided transparent tape on the bottoms of the furniture.

Modular interior layout model - gray chipboard. (1/8" scale [1:96] student project by T. Price.)

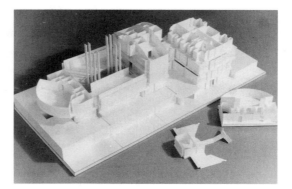

Take-apart interior model - white Strathmore. (KZF, Inc., Architects; 1/8" scale (1:96) model by C. Willis.)

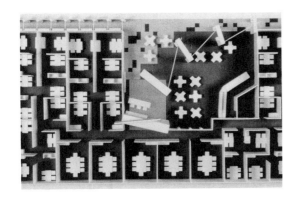

Office furniture layout. (Photo courtesy of Space Design International; 1/8" scale [1:96] model by G. Humphrey.)

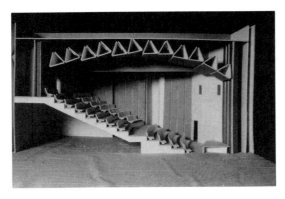

Sectional auditorium model showing configurable acoustical panels - colored illustration board. (1/4" scale [1:48] student project by A. Whittier.)

Interpretive nature center furniture layout model. (F. Moore, Architect; 1/8" scale [1:96] model by S. Johnston.)

# Chapter 8:
# MODEL PHOTOGRAPHY

Photographs of the building model provide a means of greatly expanding the audience for the model through publication. The client frequently requires photographs for news releases and publicity brochures. Photographs are easily and economically reproducible, allowing the design to be exhibited at multiple locations. Furthermore, models are fragile objects, easily damaged by physical abuse, dust, color fading, and in the case of paperboard construction by warping due to temperature and humidity changes. In addition, they are bulky and thus difficult to transport and store. By comparison, photographs of models are permanent and compact for easy transport and storage.

Photographs can enhance the reality of the model by controlling the lighting (to simulate sunlight and shadows), simulating the surrounding environment (sky, surrounding buildings), and the viewer's location (eye-level, overhead, interior, etc.). Finally, sequences of photographs (particularly slides) can be used to control the presentation of the design to the client.

In a design presentation, the very advantages inherent to a model (i.e., simultaneously revealing all aspects of the design) can make it difficult for the designer to control the attention of the client - particularly in a group meeting. How can the designer, for example, talk about the general concepts behind the elementary school design while each member of the school board is looking at a different part of the model? On first seeing the model, even the very

1/4" scale (1:48) passive solar house.
(Design and model by S. Johnston.)

quality of "miniaturization" in the model is so fascinating to many clients that it is difficult for them to concentrate on the design itself.   For that reason, many designers elect to present the design first only using slides, and delay the model unveiling until after the slide presentation.   This allows the designer to completely control the focus and pace of the presentation.

For example, the slide sequence may be used to walk the client through the building. Close-ups of the entrance would be used to accompany the designer's verbal rationale of that part of the design.   Slides of the same area of the plan drawing may be

integrated into the sequence, reinforcing the relationship between the literal image of the model and the abstract image of the plan.

## SHOOT LOCATION

Building models can be photographed outside (utilizing the natural sky, sunlight, etc.) or inside (where these conditions must be simulated). If an outdoor location is elected, weather conditions control the "shoot." If conditions are ideal, the clear sky (ideally with scattered white clouds) can be used for the sky in the photograph. Natural direct sunlight provides an ideal light source. The sun provides a point source of light producing sharp shadows. Being a virtually infinite distance away, sunlight shadows are parallel and do not converge (as they would with a nearer, artificial light). Finally, the white color of sunlight matches the color balance of most films.

A major disadvantage of the outdoor studio is the difficulty of controlling the background (out-of-scale foliage and buildings). And, of course, the ideal weather conditions necessary for outdoor model photography may not occur when needed. Invariably, design project schedules are tight, and it often becomes necessary to photograph the model when weather conditions are impossible.

An interior studio allows the model to be photographed at any time under controlled conditions. However, a number of props are required to realistically simulate the outside environment.

*Photographing a model interior.*

## SPACE AND DEPTH

Creating an illusion of space and depth in a model photograph requires "layering" the composition into zones from the front (nearest the camera) to back (furthest from the camera).

An eye-level exterior photograph should include: a foreground, a midground (usually where the building is), a background, a skyline (usually trees or adjacent buildings), and a sky backdrop.

### Foreground

In most cases, the foreground is limited to the model base; avoid showing the edge of the model base within the foreground because it completely destroys any illusion of scale and reality that the model is intended to create. A shadow across this foreground (presumably from some unseen tree or building) can be added to help break up an otherwise monotonous expanse of grass or paving. If the edge of the base is unavoidable, the shadow tends to camouflage it and minimize its impact.

Furthermore, this darker element tends to create a compositional frame across the bottom of the photograph, leading the eye to the lighter middle zone and the building beyond. These shadows can be created by the photographer holding an object (or arm) so as to cast a shadow laterally across the foreground; do not worry about holding the shadow perfectly still during the exposure - in fact, a little movement helps blur the shadow, thus softening its outline.

A "tree branch" silhouette drooping down into the photograph from an unseen tree above serves to create the same framing effect. Unlike the ground shadow, it is important that the overhead branch be sharp (and not blurred by movement). Tape the branch onto some temporary support.

*Foreground.*

## Midground

The midground should contain the building, preferably positioned at an angle so that two sides are shown. Usually, the building is angled so that the most important facade is viewed most directly and the subordinate facade shown more obliquely. This midground should receive the strongest lighting to draw attention toward the main subject.

## Background

The background is that area of the landscape behind the model but in front of those elements forming the skyline (trees, building tops, etc.). Often the model base must be extended. In an urban environment, this might require adding horizontal sheets of illustration board to extend the base. Because the angle of view of the camera for eye-level shots is so shallow, small cracks and joints are virtually unnoticeable. In addition, the lighting can be controlled in order to brightly light the building itself and leave the background much darker and thus less distinct.

For rural environments, a wrinkled blanket (an olive drab "army" blanket is ideal) gives a more undulating background and can even be sloped up to simulate hills and mountains for the skyline.

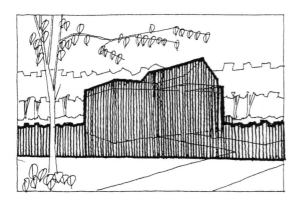

*Midground.*

*Background.*

## Horizon

The height of the skyline is very important if the horizon (by definition, always at camera level, even though hidden) is to seem natural. Make sure that the skyline (tops of background trees or buildings) is well above the height of the camera. It is a common mistake to position the camera too high relative to the horizon.

**Remember**: No sky should ever be visible below the camera level.

## Skyline

The skyline for all architectural model photographs should be above the horizon, which is the same as the camera height. Only an infinite expanse of level terrain (ocean or desert) would have a skyline that matches the horizon; virtually all other skylines - urban or rural - would be above the horizon.

Usually, the skyline (like the background) is left dark and in silhouette, minimizing the need for detail. Rural skylines can be created by supporting the wrinkled-blanket background to a height higher than the camera so that its silhouette is undulating; arrange lichen along the ridge to "break up" the smooth silhouette. For urban environments, use blocks or cardboard cutouts to create a skylinesilhouette.

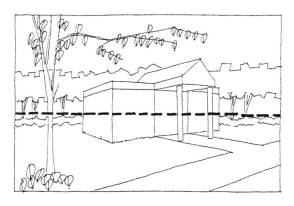

Horizon.

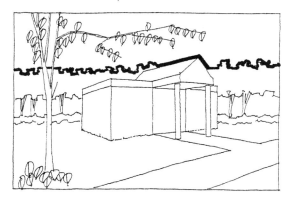

Skyline.

## Sky backdrop...
must be created for eye-level photographs of exterior models.  It should be larger than the model base - at least 8 ft wide by 8 ft tall (2.5 m x 2.5 m).

## Painted background
A comparatively low cost solution for the sky is to purchase a roll of seamless photographers' background paper (available 8 ft [2.5 m] wide). The color can be either light blue (for a cloudless sky) or white with blue added by spray painting (for a more dramatic partly cloudy sky).

Black seamless paper is also used to create contrast with a predominantly white building or to simulate night conditions.  The paper roll is supported by a horizontal rod 8 ft [2.5 m] above the floor, and the paper pulled down like a window shade for use.  After the shoot is complete, the paper is rolled back up where it is protected from dust and scuffing, leaving the studio space free for other uses.

Alternatively, if a smooth wall is available, it can be "dedicated" as a model sky and painted accordingly. However, even minor scuff marks become visible in the photograph, requiring the wall to be repainted frequently.

*Unnatural - horizon and skyline appear too low; sky visible below the height of the camera.*

*Natural - skyline above the height of camera - no sky visible below height of camera. (Design and model by Gerardo Brown-Manrique.)*

**Slide-projected background**
An alternative to painted sky backgrounds is to use a slide photograph of a real sky and project it onto a matte white background behind the model.   The projector must be positioned so that no shadows are projected (from the model, table, light stands, camera, etc.).

The best projector location is usually high and well behind the camera (a stepladder provides a convenient platform).   Make certain that the white background is completely matte or a disturbing "hot spot" reflection from the projector will occur.

The brightness of the projector can be adjusted by placing cardboard over part of the front of the lens; taping a coin over the center works better with some lenses. (See the discussion below about how to balance the brightness of the sky relative to the building.)   If necessary, shield the model from the projector by taping a cardboard "barn door" to the side of the lens.

Carefully shield the projected sky image from extraneous light from surrounding sources (for example, the "sunlight") to prevent washing out its contrast.

Sky backdrop.

## LIGHTING

Three light sources are necessary for exterior building models: sunlight, reflected fill light (to soften the shadows from the "sunlight"), and backdrop light (to illuminate the sky backdrop). Use incandescent sources for all of these (with the appropriate color film and/or color correction filter as discussed later in this chapter).

### Sunlight

One (and only one) very strong point source is used to simulate direct sunlight and create a single set of sharp shadows. The ideal artificial sunlight source is a 500- to 750-watt studio quartz light, complete with barn-door blinders (used to restrict the area of sunlight). A slide projector (without a slide) is a good alternative sun. Pieces of black cardboard taped to the side of the lens can serve as barn doors. Both of these yield very sharp shadows.

"Photoflood" incandescent bulbs (3400°K color temperature, available at camera shops) can be used, but the shadows are not as sharp because the source

size is larger. Even conventional 250-watt incandescent reflector bulbs can be used; theoretically, the warmer color of these is not recommended, but in practice they are quite acceptable for model color photography.

Fluorescent lamps are unacceptable for two reasons: they result in diffuse shadows and they have a color spectrum that is impossible to correct without very sophisticated filtration. Flash and strobe lights are not recommended because of the difficulty in previsualizing the effect of these sources on shadows and surface textures.

Quartz studio light with barn doors for simulating direct sunlight.

Three-quarter view with frontlighting (notice how "flat" the building appears).

Three-quarter view with side lighting (notice how sidelighting enhances the three-dimensionality of the shape).

**Position...**

the sun to best reveal the three-dimensional form of the building. In most cases, this is more important than positioning the source with regard to a correct solar orientation. For the typical three-quarter exterior views where two adjacent sides of the building are visible, for example, position the light off to the side directed toward the model approximately perpendicular to the camera direction. This allows the "important" side of the building (typically the entrance) to be featured in direct sunlight, and the less important side to be subordinated in shadow.

The height of the sun is also important. For eye-level photographs, use a relatively low angle to create long, dramatic building shadows on the ground, and emphasize any undulations in the landscape.

For bird's-eye photographs, where the roof is visible, it is very important to control the height so that light intensity is different on all three visible surfaces (roof and two visible facades). This is necessary to clearly distinguish the different planes. It is important in any photograph, but especially important with monochromatic mass models where color differences are not available to help distinguish planes. As a general rule, position the light source so that

the light strikes each of the visible surfaces at markedly different angles.

The further the sun can be positioned away from the model, the more uniform the illumination over the entire model base. While this uniformity is usually desirable, a modest concentration of light on the building itself will focus attention there while increasing the feeling of depth in eye-level shots.

*Poor: Front lighting - all three surfaces lighted equally.*

*Better: top and left side lighted equally, right side in shade.*

*Best: all three surfaces lighted differently (notice how this creates the contrast necessary to reveal the three-dimensionality of the form).*

**Diffuse sky light**

If the sunlight point source is the only illumination of the model, the shadow and shade areas become very dark and "opaque," resulting in a very contrasty photograph. In reality, direct sunlight is supplemented by diffuse light from the entire sky vault as well as sunlight reflected from clouds, surrounding buildings, and the ground. The effect of all of this diffuse "fill" light is to soften the harsh shadows created by sunlight.

This fill light can be easily created by the use of a diffuse reflector. Position a sheet of white illustration board directly opposite the sun source just

outside the view of the camera. The light reflected will soften the shadows from the sun. Do not use a second light, as this will create unnatural double shadows.

**Sky backdrop lighting**

If a seamless paper or painted sky backdrop is used (instead of a slide projected sky), it should be lighted separately from the model. The best arrangement is to position two or more incandescent lamps on the floor shining up on the sky backdrop. This creates a gradation of sky brightness, being brightest near the horizon and becoming darker near the top. This makes for a dramatic photograph with the dark blue sky overhead with the building silhouetted against the lighter horizon.

Position the sun to create oblique ("grazing") light to emphasize texture and reveals on the facade.

Using an illustration board reflector for diffuse fill light.

Without reflector fill light (notice how dense and opaque the shadows are).

## VIEWPOINT

The vertical height of the camera relative to the model is an important consideration. It affects the relative importance of the roof versus the facade, the visibility of the sky, the apparent height of the observer, and the height of the horizon.

### Worm's-eye...

or ground-level views are visually dramatic, but unnatural in appearance, and reveal little about the three-dimensional form of the building.

### Eye-level...

photographs represent the view that a person would actually see while walking (or driving) toward the building. It is the most realistic simulation of how the completed building will be viewed by its users.

*Worm's-eye view.*

*Eye-level view.*

### Low-level bird's-eye...

views are above eye level, typically show some of the roof surface, but are still low enough so that the horizon (always at camera height) is still visible within the frame of the camera. This greatly complicates the simulation of the background and skyline, which are completely exposed above the building. For this reason, low-level bird's-eye views are often avoided.

### High-level bird's-eye...

views show the roof more directly and are sufficiently high so that the horizon is well above the frame of the camera and no part of the sky is visible. This view is often used for buildings with unusual roof forms because the roof becomes the dominant surface of the building. In addition this view clearly shows the shape of the building. It is easy to inadvertently tilt the camera to one side when shooting bird's-eye views, resulting in the buildings appearing to tilt in the finished photo. Make sure that building verticals in the center of the scene are parallel with the sides of the viewfinder.

### Plan...

views are the ultimate high-angle bird's-eye view - directly overhead. Because it is difficult to support the camera directly over the model, it is usually more convenient to tilt the model while mounting the camera on a tall tripod. Make sure that the film plane of the camera is parallel to the model base to prevent perspective convergence distortion in the final photograph.

*High-level bird's-eye view - church. (IPG, Inc., Architects; 1" = 60' scale [1:720] model by J. Ingram and R. Hill.)*

*Plan view - vocational school complex. (IPG, Inc., Architects; 1" = 50' scale [1:600] model by J. Ingram.)*

## Interior view

The roof or ceiling of most interior
models is removable to allow the client
to view the interior directly from above
with a minimum disturbance to the
remainder of the model.    Although it is
possible to utilize viewing ports in the
walls of the model,   these invariably
result in viewing distances that are too
close for comfortable focusing.
Photographs are especially important
for interior models because they can
show the interior from controlled
viewpoints that are neither comfortable
nor convenient for the client to utilize in
viewing the model directly.

*Photographing interior model with
removable end wall section.*

*Model interior photographed from
removable end wall.*

## CAMERAS

**Single-lens reflex 35-mm cameras** are the most versatile choice for model photography because: (1) they are compact and relatively inexpensive, (2) the view through the viewfinder matches the view recorded on film, (3) they accept wide-angle, interchangeable lenses, (4) most incorporate a through-the-lens meter, and (5) a wide selection of films is available.

**View cameras...** are preferred by professional photographers for architectural photography. Their large negative size permits the sharpest possible enlargements, and the adjustments possible with this bellows camera allow complete control over the perspective of the final photograph. However, their physical size and completely manual operation, their unsuitability for making slide photographs, and the special film processing required make view cameras less suited for use by design professionals for model photography.

**Special periscope cameras...** are available which allow eye-level photography in otherwise inaccessible model locations. These cameras use instant film, allowing immediate access to color and black-and-white prints.

View camera - the front lens may be raised to control perspective distortion.

Periscope-type model camera. (Photograph courtesy of Charrette, Inc.)

Photograph made using periscope-type model camera. (Courtesy of Charrette, Inc.)

## FILM

If a tripod is available (highly recommended), then a fine-grain, slow-speed film (ASA 32 to 100) is recommended.   If extremely low light levels necessitate exposures longer than five seconds with color film, a slight color shift may result from "reciprocity failure."   This may be avoided where color balance is critical by using a faster film speed.

If color slide film is used, the type color-balanced for the tungsten light source should be used (for example, Kodak Ektachrome 160 ASA type B slide film).   Standard (daylight-balanced) slide film will appear orangish if photographed using incandescent (or quartz) lights; compensate for this by using a 80B blue color conversion filter.

In general, color prints can be made from slides by most photoprocessing laboratories, but these are of poorer quality (higher contrast and grainier) and more expensive than prints from original color negative film (for example, Kodak Kodacolor 100 ASA). Similarly, black-and-white prints made from color slides (usually via an internegative) are poorer than those made from either black-and-white or color negatives.   Custom labs can prepare high quality slides from color negatives; these are typically better than slide duplicates.

Motion picture films (35 mm, such as Kodak 5293/5247 and Fuji 8518) are available spooled for use in 35-mm still cameras from mail-order photo-processing labs (see photography magazine advertisements); when returned for processing, these films yield both high-quality color negatives and color slides at modest cost.

## EXPOSURE

For exterior models, the contrast range is comparatively low and the camera meter will typically produce satisfactory results. However, determining exposure for model interiors, like building interiors, is difficult because of the extreme brightness range between the window openings and shadowed interior areas.

The exposure latitude of any film is much shorter than the human eye. Extremely bright areas, such as the sky and surrounding exterior, tend to completely dominate the camera meter. Invariably, if these areas are visible within the sensitivity zone of the camera meter, the interior will be underexposed.

When taking the exposure reading, aim the camera so that the window (or any light source) is just out of the field of view. Set the exposure, and then return to the desired view to take the photograph. (Automatic exposure modes are typically unsuccessful; use the manual mode on automatic cameras.) If the interior model surfaces are very light in color, then exposure should be about one extra f-stop greater to avoid underexposure.

At best, exposure for all model photographs is an art. Even technically correct exposures frequently fail to represent the view as perceived by the eye. Because of this, it is recommended that exposures be "bracketed" two f-stops over and two f-stops under. If an automatic camera is used that does not have a manual mode, change the ASA film speed settings for each shot in order to bracket - doubling the ASA equals one f-stop underexposure; halving the ASA equals one f-stop overexposure, etc. In either case, the extra cost of the film "wasted" in bracketing is negligible compared with the inconvenience and time wasted in having to reshoot.

## LENSES

For exterior models, normal (50-mm) to moderate wide angle (35-mm) lenses are recommended to produce a pleasing perspective. Moderate telephotos (85- to 135-mm) are well suited for bird's eye views, but make the building perspective look "flat" when used for eye-level shots. Conversely, wide and ultrawide lenses exaggerate the depth and perspective convergence of building exteriors so dramatically that they should be reserved for special effects only. Furthermore, the wide coverage of these lenses requires the use of a much larger sky background.

For interiors, however, wide- to ultrawide-angle lenses (18- to 28-mm) are usually required to provide the necessary coverage of the interior when the camera location is very close (for example, through a small viewing port in the side of the model). In addition, these wide-angle lenses have an inherently greater depth of focus as well as a closer minimum focusing distance - two desirable characteristics for the circumstances of interior model photography.

If the only camera access to the interior is from a small viewing port, then very wide angle lenses (18- to 28-mm) are usually necessary to get full coverage of the room. The wide coverage of lenses in the 18- to 28-mm range comes with a penalty of an apparent distortion of depth in the final photograph - the room will appear much deeper than it really is (the wider the lens, the greater this distortion). Furthermore, objects near the edge of the photograph will appear distorted in shape. Circles, for example, will appear elliptical. Surprisingly, the reason for this apparent distortion is not the lens itself, but the distance from the camera to the subject (in this case very short). See Moore, 1976, for a more complete discussion of the perception of depth in architectural photography.

Exaggerated perspective - eye-level exterior taken with 28-mm wide-angle lens.

Normal perspective - eye-level exterior taken with 35-mm moderate wide-angle lens.

Flat perspective - eye-level exterior taken with 105-mm telephoto lens.

The only way to reduce this depth distortion while maintaining adequate coverage of the room is to increase the distance from the camera to the subject (by removing the entire wall) and using a moderate-wide-angle lens (i.e., 35-mm). While this creates an "impossible" viewpoint (outside the room), in practice, this anomaly goes unnoticed, and the result is a pleasing perspective that realistically represents the spatial character of the interior. Be careful to not let unwanted sunlight enter through the removed wall opening; temporary shielding may be necessary.

*Model interior photographed from a wall port using a 35-mm lens - realistic depth but coverage is too narrow.*

*Same interior photographed from same wall port using 20-mm ultra-wide-angle lens - good coverage but depth appears greatly exaggerated.*

*Compare with same interior photographed from greater distance (entire wall removed) using 35-mm lens realistic depth and good coverage.*

## DEPTH OF FIELD...

is the area of the model that is in focus. It is usually desirable to have the greatest area of the model possible in sharp focus. This requires great depth of field that can be achieved only by using the smallest possible lens aperture setting. The aperture settings on a typical wide-angle lens range from f3.5 (widest aperture, narrowest depth of field) to f22 (smallest aperture, greatest depth of field).

This great depth of field is only available at a price. Small apertures restrict the amount of light entering through the lens. In order to get sufficient light onto the film to expose it properly, a long exposure (slow shutter speed setting) is required. Even with 500-watt quartz lighting, exposures of one second or longer are common. A tripod and cable release are necessary for these long exposures.

"Hand-holding" the camera is not recommended and is only possible with shutter speeds of one-sixtieth and faster. These high shutter speeds are possible by using a large aperture and/or fast (high ASA number) film. The results are usually mediocre with grainy enlargements and the front and/or back of the building being out of focus.

### Focusing

Focus the camera on a piece of the model that is one-third back between the closest point of the building and the furthest visible point on the building. This optimizes the field of focus so that the entire building is in sharp focus.

Wide aperture (f3.5) results in short exposure time and shallow depth of field (notice that center zone is sharp but front and back are out of focus).

Narrow aperture opening (f32) results in long exposure time and great depth of field (notice that the building is in sharp focus from front to back).

## PERSPECTIVE CONTROL

If the camera is tilted up (or down), the vertical edges of the model will converge. While this is an optically correct perspective effect, it is made particularly noticeable and distracting because of the presence of the parallel sides of the photograph. This problem is most common with tall exterior models; it occurs in interior models only in cases where the room is very tall or when the ceiling is particularly dominant. It is further exaggerated with wide-angle lenses. This convergence can be controlled in several ways.

One way is to use a wider angle lens from the same camera position. Rotate the camera so that the long side of the frame is vertical. Now the top of the building is visible, and (because the camera is not tilted) vertical model edges are parallel. The bottom of the image will contain a large area of (uninteresting) foreground; this should be cropped from the final print or masked from the final slide.

Another alternative is to use the same lens and move further from the model to include the top of the building (and more foreground) while not tilting the camera. The procedure is otherwise the same as above. This use of a longer lens will make the perspective of the photograph look flatter.

The ideal solution is to shift the lens vertically. This allows the top of the building to be included without tilting the camera. View cameras have this capability, as discussed previously. Special perspective control (PC) lenses are available for 35-mm cameras which have this same shifting capability. They are expensive and available from most of the major camera manufacturers in 35-mm moderate-wide-angle and 28-mm wide-angle focal lengths.

Tilting the camera up (or down) creates a converging perspective "keystone" effect.

No camera tilt - verticals are parallel but top is missing.

No camera tilt (verticals parallel) with lens shifted up (top is visible).

Of the two, the 35-mm PC lens is recommended for both architectural model photography as well as general architectural photography. The capabilities of the more extreme 28-mm (or in the case of one manufacturer, 24-mm) PC lens is needed only for very tall subjects where the camera-to-subject distance is limited by some obstruction. In all other circumstances, the 35-mm lens is preferred because it produces less perspective distortion and depth exaggeration (due to the greater camera-to-subject distance).

35-mm camera with special perspective control lens in shifted position up to maintain parallel verticals.

# REFERENCES

Burden, E., 1971, *Architectural Delineation: A Photographic Approach.* New York: McGraw-Hill.

Charrette, Inc., 1989, *Catalog.* P. O. Box 4010, Woburn, MA 01888-4010

Cowan, H., et. al, 1968, **Models in Architecture.** New York: Elsevier.

McClanahan, B., 1976, *Scenery for Model Railroads.* Milwaukee: Kalmbach Books.

Moore, F., 1976, "Perceptual Distortion of Space in 2D Architectural Media," chapter in **Drawing Skills in Architecture** by McGinty, T., Dubuque: Kendall Hunt, pp. 120-132.

Moore, F., 1985, *Concepts and Practice of Architectural Daylighting.* New York: Van Nostrand-Reinhold.

Schiler, M., editor, 1987, *Daylighting Models.* Los Angeles: Department of Architecture, University of Southern California.

Warren, B., 1975, *764 Hints for Model Railroaders.* Milwaukee: Kalmbach Books.

# Appendix A:
# RECIPES FOR RENDERING BUILDING MATERIALS

The markers specified in this appendix refer to Berol Prismacolor Art Marker designations. The colored pencils refer to Berol Prismacolor pencils.   See Appendix C for a table cross-referencing marker colors by various manufacturers.

## BRICK  MASONRY

Surface:    Strathmore  board  or  paper
Markers:    red brick: Dark Tan PM-94
            buff brick: Lt. Walnut PM-95
Graphite pencil: 2H
Tempera:  mortar: cream
Colored pencil: mortar: 964 Gray

### 1/8" scale  (1:96)  and  smaller
Begin with a uniform "wash" of wide horizontal marker strokes applied using a parallel bar straightedge. Try not to overlap or leave gaps in the strokes. The color of the marker should be the lightest color of the brick face. (For 1" = 20' [1:240] scale and smaller, do

not attempt to show horizontal or vertical mortar joints; stop at this point. )

Next, using an architectural scale, measure off the vertical spacing of the horizontal mortar joints at 3 courses per 8" [20 cm]. Do not try to estimate

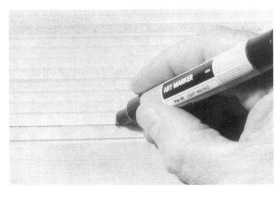

Brick at 1/8" scale (1:96): uniform wash of brick colored marker using wide tip against parallel bar.

Brick at 1/8" scale (1:96): carefully lay out the mortar joint spacing at 3 per 8" and draft using sharp pencil.

Brick at 1/8" scale (1:96): darken random courses using fine marker.

this spacing because brick coursing is familiar to most people and gives a strong indication of building scale. Making the brick spacing larger by even 20% will result in the building appearing that same percentage smaller than designed.

At 1/8" scale (1:96), it is difficult to draw white or light gray joints sufficiently fine (a line representing a 3/8" [10 mm] mortar joint would have to be .003" [0.1 mm] to appear natural) ; instead, "suggest" the coursing by drawing horizontal pencil lines using a sharp 2H lead at the correct spacing.   Do not show any vertical joints.

Finally, using a fine point marker (same color as the original),  apply a second "coat" to darken brick courses.  Try to make these as narrow as a single course; extend across the entire width of masonry.

### 3/16" to 3/8" scale (1:64 - 1:32)

Again, begin with a uniform "wash" of brick-colored marker, and lay out the horizontal mortar joints and a sprinkling of individual bricks. Using the same marker, darken these random bricks with a second coat to give a "range" to the bricks.

Draw the horizontal mortar joints using either medium or light gray tempera

(too much contrast here makes the joints dominate the facade) in a ruling pen, or very sharp white colored pencil. (Vertical joints are optional. )

### 1/2" scale (1:24) and larger

Repeat the above sequence; include the vertical joints.  Finally, using a sharp 2H pencil, add shadow lines below and to one side of the brick.

Brick at 1/4" scale (1:48): darken random individual bricks using same marker.

Brick at 1" scale (1:12): draft shadow lines across the bottom and one side of individual bricks.

## STIPPLE-TEXTURED SURFACES (gravel, grass, stucco, carpeting, etc.)

Surface:   colored illustration board or paper

Tempera:   light and darker shades of surface base color

Applicator: mouth atomizer (or toothbrush rubbed on insect screen)

### All scales

For large areas, create a uniform base color using pastels applied with cotton, or colored paper, or paint, etc. Next, apply one or more very light spray applications of colored tempera using the mouth atomizer.

Thin the tempera to the consistency of milk. Let each spray application dry before applying the next. For texture only (no overall color change), make the first spray a darker shade of the base color and the second a lighter shade of the same color. For strong textures, contrast the colors of these sprays greatly; for a more subtle effect, use less contrast.

To shift the overall color of the surface, use complementary colors for the various sprays. For example, to create grass texture over a light olive-green base, spray light applications of yellow-green, brown-green, and blue-green. This will add a richness and realism to an otherwise flat, monotonous surface.

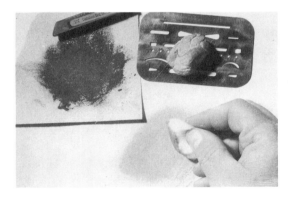

Textured surfaces - grind stick pastel into powder and apply using cotton ball.

Textured surfaces - applying a tempera spray texture to a painted model base using a mouth atomizer.

Textured surfaces - closeup showing spray texture.

## CUT LIMESTONE, UNPAINTED CONCRETE BLOCK

Surface: Strathmore board or paper

Markers: limestone: Putty PM-80
        block: 20% Warm Gray PM-102

Graphite pencil: 2H lead

Tempera: limestone: white and light
        warm gray
      concrete block: light and
        dark gray

Tempera lines: mortar: light warm gray

Applicators: mouth atomizer, ruling pen

**All scales**

Begin with a uniform "wash" of wide horizontal marker strokes applied using a parallel bar straightedge. Try not to overlap or leave gaps in the strokes. The color of the marker should be the lightest color of the material. Next, draft the joints of any units taller (or wider) than 8" (20 cm) using a sharp 2H pencil. Next, slightly darken random units with a second coat of the same marker.

Finally, at scales greater than 1/2" = 1'-0" (1:24), add light-gray mortar joints with ruling pen and tempera. Add a spray texture of white and light warm gray tempera.

*Limestone at 1/4" scale (1:48): uniform wash of very light marker using wide tip against parallel bar.*

*Limestone at 1/4" scale (1:48): draft pencil joints; darken random stones with second coat of marker.*

# FIELD STONE MASONRY

Surface: Strathmore board or paper

Markers: mortar: Putty PM-80
        light stone: 30% Warm Gray
        accent stones:
            Light Tan PM-95
            Sand PM-70
        shadow:  50% Warm Gray

### 1/8" scale (1:96) and smaller
Begin with a uniform "wash" of wide horizontal 20% Warm Gray marker strokes applied using a parallel bar straightedge. Try not to overlap or leave gaps in the strokes. The color of the marker should be the color of the lightest stones. Next, draw individual stones using a combination of freehand and drafting with a soft graphite pencil (B or 2B lead). At this small scale, do not attempt to draw every stone for very large areas. To suggest shadows, draw the top and one side of the stones very lightly and the bottom and other side darker. Finally, add second coat to random stones using fine point markers of two or three different colors.

### 3/16" to 3/8" scale (1:64 - 1:32)
Begin with a uniform "wash" of wide horizontal marker strokes applied using a parallel bar straightedge. Try not to overlap or leave gaps in the strokes.

The color of the marker should be the color of the mortar joints. Draw the outline of each stone freehand using a soft, graphite pencil. Keep the joints narrow, and make each stone seem to almost fit to the previous one without making extreme concavities in any single stone. To create a suggestion of shadow on the recessed mortar, draw the bottoms and one side of the stones darker that the tops and opposite side.

### 1/2" scale (1:24) and larger
At this scale, field stone is rendered similar to the above, except that a 50% Warm Gray fine-tip marker is used to shadow the bottom and one side of the stone to increase its apparent relief.

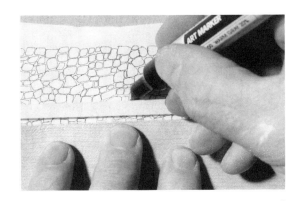

Field stone at 1/8" scale (1:96): draw outline of stones with waterproof ink (black or gray) or pencil and apply light marker wash.

Field stone at 1/8" scale (1:96): darken random stones with second coat.

Field stone at 1/2" scale (1:24): use a fine-point marker to suggest shadows on bottom and one side of individual stones.

# WOOD SIDING and PANELING

Surface:  Strathmore board or paper

Markers:  redwood: Light Tan PM-95
cedar:  Putty PM-80
contrasting trim (second
coat): 40% Warm Gray
light oak: Sand PM-70
dark oak: Walnut PM-88
mahogany: Light Tan PM-95
teak: Burnt Ochre PM-66
birch: Sand PM-70
rosewood: Light Tan PM-66
shadows (second coat):
50% Warm Gray PM-103

Graphite pencil: graining and joints: 2H

## 1/8" scale (1:96) and smaller

Begin with a uniform "wash" of wide marker strokes applied in the direction of the wood grain and joints using a straightedge. Try not to overlap or leave gaps in the strokes. The color of the marker should be the lightest color of the material.

Next, draft the joints at the correct spacing using a 2H sharp pencil. For bevel-edge (lapped) siding, make the pencil lines dark to suggest a shadow on the underside of each board. Finally, slightly darken random boards with a second coat of the same marker. Do not try to add any "grain."

## 3/16" to 3/8" scale (1:64 - 1:32)

Similar to above, except draft stronger shadow line joints of lapped siding using a gray (diluted black) ink with a ruling pen or technical drawing pen. This scale is still too small to show wood grain.

## 1/2" scale (1:24) and larger

Similar to the above except, for bevel-edge siding, add an additional shadow line of 50% Warm Gray fine-line marker just below the joint line. If the grain pattern is particularly pronounced, add linework using a sharp colored pencil in darker and lighter shades of the base stroke. Keep graining very subdued so that it does not dominate the surface visually.

Wood siding - after drafting detail on white five-ply illustration board, apply color using broad marker and straightedge.

Wood siding - color with marker over inked siding and window frames.

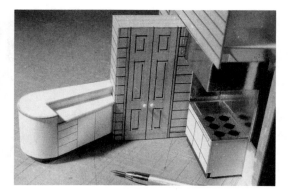

For wood trim, panel doors, etc., draft shadow lines only to suggest three-dimensional relief.

# SHINGLES (roofing, siding)

Surface: Strathmore board or paper

Markers: cedar:  Putty PM-80
    contrasting trim (second coat):
        50% Warm Gray PM-103
    asphalt shingles: to match
        selected shingle color
    shadows (second coat):
        50% Warm Gray PM-103

Graphite pencil: joints: 2H (or gray ink)

## 1/8" scale (1:96) and smaller

Begin with a uniform "wash" of horizontal wide marker strokes applied using a straightedge. Try not to overlap or leave gaps in the strokes. The color of the marker should be the lightest color of the material. Measure and draft the joints at the correct spacing. To show the joints and a small shadow line, use a sharp 2H pencil over light marker; dark gray or black ink over dark marker. Do not show any vertical joints at this scale.

## 3/16" to 3/8" scale (1:64 - 1:32)

Similar to the above, except draft stronger shadow line joints of wood shingles using a gray (diluted black) ink with a ruling pen or technical drawing pen. Add random vertical joints using a light pencil and straightedge. Slightly darken random individual shingles with a second coat of the original marker color (use a fine marker point if available) to show the range inherent in these small individual units. This scale is still too small to show wood grain.

## 1/2" scale (1:24) and larger

Similar to the above, except show all vertical lines with thin pencil.

For thick hand-split shakes, add an additional shadow line of 50% Warm Gray fine-line marker just below the horizontal joint line. For heavy, hand-split cedar shakes, draw this marker shadow line carefully freehand with a slight "jerkiness" to suggest the varying thickness of this material.

*Shingles at 1/4" scale (1:48) and larger - draw vertical joints lightly in pencil and second coat random shingles with original marker color.*

*Hand-split cedar shakes at 1/2" scale (1:24) and larger - add "jerky" shadow line to suggest variations in thickness.*

# GLOSSY SOLID COLORS

Surface:     white Strathmore or colored illustration board or paper

Pastel:      base color of material (grind into powder with sandpaper)

Graphite pencil: dark joints: 2H (or gray ink)

Tempera:     light joints: light shade of base color

Applicator: cotton balls (for applying pastel powder)

Gloss:       clear plastic sheet overlay

**Any scale**

Begin with a uniformly colored surface. For small areas, uniform coloring can be quickly applied using pastels. Grind the pastel into a powder using fine sandpaper, and apply the powder to white illustration board.

For darker or stronger colors, apply the pastel directly to the illustration board and smooth using cotton balls. If the application of the pastel is thick, stabilize it by spraying with two light coats of workable fixative.

For larger areas, it is usually easier to purchase a sheet of paper of illustration board in the desired color.

(Watercolor and tempera paints are not recommended due to their tendency to cause warping.)

To add gloss to the surface, apply a sheet of pressure-sensitive clear laminating plastic.

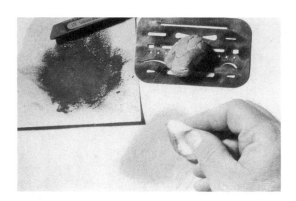

*Solid colors - apply pastel color to illustration board using cotton ball.*

# WOOD FLOORING

Surface: Strathmore board or paper

Markers: oak or maple: Sand PM-70

Graphite pencil: graining and joints: 2H

Semi-gloss: contact vinyl cover sheet

## Any scale

Begin with a uniform "wash" of wide marker strokes applied in the direction of the wood flooring using a straightedge. Try not to overlap or leave gaps in the strokes. The color of the marker should be the lightest color of the flooring. Measure and draft the long joints at the correct spacing using a 2H sharp pencil.

At 3/8" = 1'-0" (1:32) scale and larger only, add end joints with pencil. Sightly darken random boards with a second coat of the same marker. Since most flooring is a premium grade wood, do not show any individual grain.

Apply a sheet of clear, pressure-sensitive plastic (use "contact vinyl" for semigloss, "laminating plastic" for high gloss). Cut an oversize piece, strip off the backing sheet, and lay over the area to be covered. Rub the plastic down lightly, and trim away the excess using a utility knife.

Burnish the plastic by temporarily covering it with a sheet of scrap paper and rubbing it with a flat edge (such as the edge of a drafting triangle). This will eliminate air pockets and ensure a good bond between the plastic and underlying surface. Do not use a small object for burnishing; it will leave impressions in the plastic that will distort its reflections.

Finally, for large scales, "score" the joints with a stylus (or empty ball point pen). This will break up the reflections of the large area into individual flooring planks to create a very realistic appearance.

Wood flooring - color the flooring with marker color Strathmore board; define joints with 2H pencil.

Wood flooring - add semigloss by covering flooring with semigloss, pressure-sensitive vinyl contact sheet.

## CERAMIC TILE

Surface:   Strathmore board or paper

Markers:   colors to match tile color

Tempera:   grout color (usually a very light shade of the tile color)

Applicator: Ruling pen (for applying thin tempera grout lines)

High gloss: pressure-sensitive laminating plastic sheet

Semigloss: pressure-sensitive contact vinyl cover sheet

### 1/4" scale (1:48) and larger

Lay out the joints in pencil, dark enough to be seen after the application of marker. Apply a uniform wash of marker using a straightedge. Using the same marker, apply a second coat to darken random tiles.

Draw the grout joints between the tiles using a ruling pen and straightedge to apply tan tempera.

To give the tile its characteristic high gloss, apply clear, high-gloss pressure-sensitive "laminating sheets." Cut an oversize piece, strip off the backing sheet, and lay over the area to be covered. Rub the plastic down lightly,

and trim away excess using a utility knife. Burnish the plastic by temporarily covering it with a sheet of scrap paper, and rubbing it with a flat edge (such as the edge of a drafting triangle). This will eliminate air pockets and insure a good bond between the plastic and underlying surface. Do not use a small object for burnishing; it will leave impressions in the plastic that will distort its reflections.

Finally, for large scales, "score" the grout lines with a stylus (or empty ball point pen). This will break up the reflections of the large area into individual tiles to create a very realistic appearance.

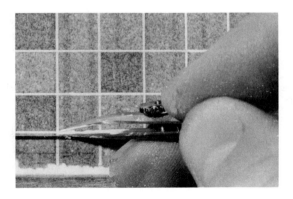

Ceramic tile - apply a uniform wash of marker and darken random tiles with a second coat of marker.

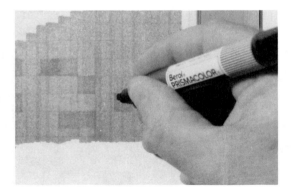

Ceramic tile - rule the grout joints with tempera.

Ceramic tile - cover the rendered tiles with laminating plastic and score the grout joints with a stylus.

# FABRICS, UPHOLSTERY, and CARPET

Surface:    Strathmore board, paper, or carved balsa

Markers:    colors to match fabric color

Tempera:    fabric color (use for stripes and tartan plaids)

Applicator: ruling pen (for straight lines) atomizer (for texture)

**Any scale**

Do not attempt to use real fabric in the model. The woven texture of even the finest cloth will appear out of scale. Furthermore, it is almost impossible to get suspended fabric (such as draperies) to hang in realistic folds; real model fabric is invariably too stiff to assume the graceful curves of its full-size counterpart. Instead, carve upholstered furniture cushions out of plaster, balsa, or foam board and paint them with tempera (for further discussion of furniture, see Appendix B: Furniture).

Model drapery with colored paper appropriately "soft-creased" to create the pleats and folds.

Wall-to-wall carpeting at a small scale should be made of colored paper. At larger scales, texture with tempera using a mouth atomizer to apply light and darker tones of the base color. If the carpeting has a repetitive pattern, carve a simple "stamp" out of the end of a piece of dowel to suggest the pattern. Coat the end of the "stamp" with tempera and press it onto the carpeting surface.

Small area rugs can be made of white paper (or given a thicker appearance using white illustration board) and colored with marker. A slight texturing can be added to any of these surfaces by spraying a light application of tempera in a color to exactly match the base material color.

Handwoven rug made of marker-colored bond paper; edge fringe is drawn with pencil.

# PATTERNED WALL COVERING

Surface:   Strathmore board, or paper

Pastel:   any background color

Tempera:   any color (use for stripes and repetitive patterns)

Applicator: cotton ball (for pastels)
ruling pen (for tempera lines)
atomizer (tempera stipple)
balsa block stamp (for repetitive patterns)

**3/8" scale (1:32) and larger**
Begin by creating a uniformly colored background surface. For small background areas, uniform coloring can be quickly applied using pastels. Grind the pastel into a powder using fine sandpaper, and apply the powder to white illustration board. For darker or stronger colors, apply the pastel directly to the illustration board and smooth using cotton balls. If the application of pastel is thick, stabilize it by spraying with two light coats of workable fixative. For larger areas, it is usually easier to purchase a sheet of paper or illustration board in the desired color. (Watercolor and tempera are not recommended for large areas due to their tendency to warp illustration board.) It is important to keep the pattern of the wall covering subdued by minimizing the contrast between applied patterns and the background. This will prevent the wall covering from visually dominating the model room interior. Apply pattern to the background by any appropriate means.

Draw linear patterns (stripes, tartan plaids) by using tempera applied with a ruling pen. Apply a tempera stipple texture using a mouth atomizer. If the wall covering has a repetitive pattern, carve a simple "stamp" out of the end of a piece of dowel to suggest the pattern. Coat the end of the "stamp" with tempera and press onto the wall covering surface.

Applying pattern to wall covering using a hardwood "stamp."

# Appendix B:
# MODEL FURNITURE DESIGNS

Detailed furniture can be very time consuming in model construction especially if exact replication of particular furniture designs is intended. Chairs, with four separate legs, can be especially tedious.

Instead, it is usually preferable to furnish the model with comparatively abstract, neutral pieces. This provides the needed indication of furniture arrangement and gives a feeling of scale and spatial definition without committing to specific furniture selection (frequently not determined at the time the client first sees the model). It allows the designer to supplement the model presentation with manufacturer's photographs or designer sketches of the furniture selected.

The following are examples of such "neutral" furniture designs that can be easily modeled using white illustration board for smaller scales and foam board at larger scales.

**Illustration board construction**
Apply any color to illustration board prior to cutting using marker. After cutting, color the white edges with marker prior to gluing.

**Foam board construction**
Cut out all pieces. Round sharp corners to resemble upholstered cushions if desired. If painting is intended, seal the exposed foam edges by "wiping" across them with latex spackling compound using the fingers. Paint with tempera.

3/8" scale (1:32) living room group.

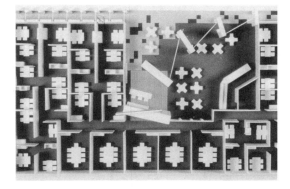

Office furniture layout. (Photo courtesy of Space Design International; 1/8" scale [1:96] model by G. Humphrey.)

Commercially available model furniture (plastic painted matte white; see Charrette, Inc.).

## Club chair

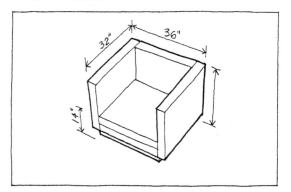

Club chair (3/8" scale [1:32]; foam board, unsealed edges, unpainted).

## Club sofa

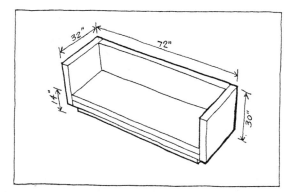

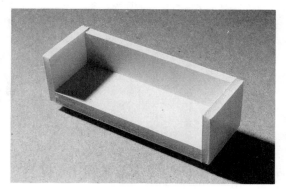

Club sofa (3/8" scale [1:32]; foam board, unsealed edges, unpainted).

## Side chair

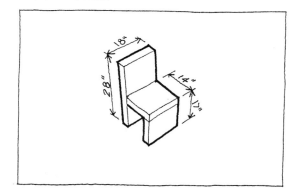

Side chair (3/8" scale [1:32]; foam board, unsealed edges, unpainted).

## Conference or dining table

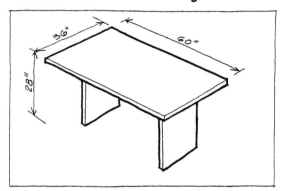

Conference desk or dining table (3/8" scale [1:32]; illustration board, marker-colored).

## Dining chair

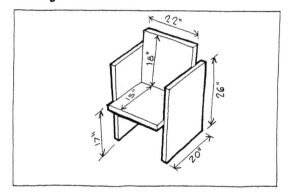

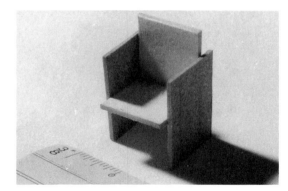

Dining chair (3/8" scale [1:32]; illustration board, marker colored).

## Coffee table

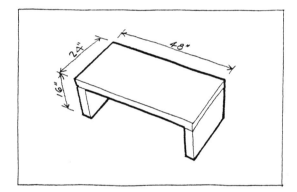

Coffee table (3/8" scale [1:32]; foam board, unsealed edges, unpainted).

## End table

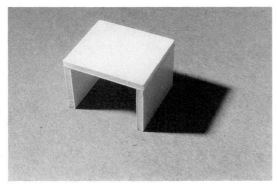

End table (3/8" scale [1:32]; foam board, unsealed edges, unpainted).

## Secretarial desk

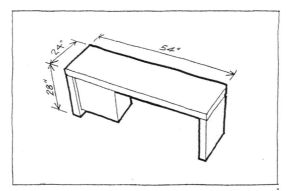

Secretarial desk (3/8" scale [1:32]; foam board, unsealed edges, unpainted).

## Executive desk

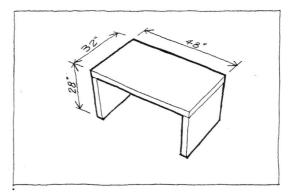

Executive desk (3/8" scale [1:32]; foam board, unsealed edges, unpainted).

# MARKER COLOR RECOMMENDATIONS

The following marker color recommendations are for the base coat on white illustration board or paper. Additional colors may be overlaid to create the grain or "range" inherent in the real material. The catalog numbers for three different manufacturers are given for each material (Berol Prismacolor Art Markers, Eberhard Faber Design Art Markers, and Chartpac Ad Markers). Because color and intensity depend on the age of the marker and the paper surface, always test the color on a scrap piece of board before applying to the model.

|  | PRISMACOLOR | DESIGN | CHARTPAC |
|---|---|---|---|
| **EXTERIOR WOODS** |  |  |  |
| Cedar, Pine, Poplar | Putty PM-80 | Brown-0  213-LO | Maize P-133 |
| Redwood | Light Tan PM-95 | Sahara Tan  443-L | Suntan P-140 |
| **INTERIOR WOODS** |  |  |  |
| Oak (light), Maple, Birch, Pine | Sand PM-70 | Beige 423-L | Beige P-137 |
| Oak (dark), Walnut | Walnut PM-88 | Brown 293-L | Sepia P-56 |
| Cherry, Mahogany, Rosewood | Light Tan PM-95 | Sahara Tan  443-L | Suntan P-140 |
| Teak, Pecan | Burnt Ochre PM-66 | Sahara Tan  443-L | Mocha P-70 |
| **MASONRY MATERIALS** |  |  |  |
| Red Brick, Quarry Tile | Dark Tan PM-94 | Calif Redwood 373-L | Desert Tan P-146 |
| Buff Brick | Light Walnut PM-89 | Beige 423-L | Beige P-137 |
| Concrete Block, Field Stone | 40% Warm Grey PM-102 | Warm Grey 5 209-L5 | Warm Grey 3 P-183 |
| Limestone, Concrete, Mortar | Putty PM-80 | Warm Grey 5 209-L5 | Warm Grey 3 P-183 |
| Slate | 80% Cool Grey PM-115 | Blue Black 365-L | Slate Blue P-97 |
| Granite | 40% Warm Grey PM-102 | Warm Grey 5 209-L5 | Warm Grey 3 P-183 |
| **METALS** |  |  |  |
| Stainless Steel | 20% Cool Grey PM-109 | Grey-2 229-L2 | Cool Grey 1 P-181 |
| Aluminum | 20% Warm Grey PM-100 | Warm Grey-4 209-L4 | Warm Grey 2 P-192 |
| Bronze, Corten Steel | Burnt Umber PM-61 | Saddle Brown P-59 | Burnt Umber P-71 |

# Appendix D:
# BUILDING EXAMPLE DESIGN DRAWINGS

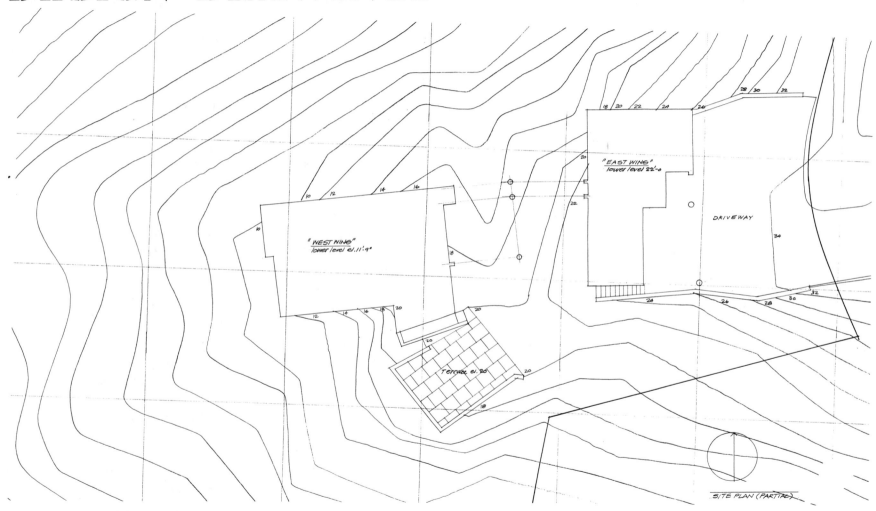

"EAST WING"
lower level 22'-0

DRIVEWAY

"WEST WING"
lower level el.11'-9"

Terrace el. 20

SITE PLAN (PARTIAL)

Private residence design drawings. (Courtesy Briner/Strain Architects.)

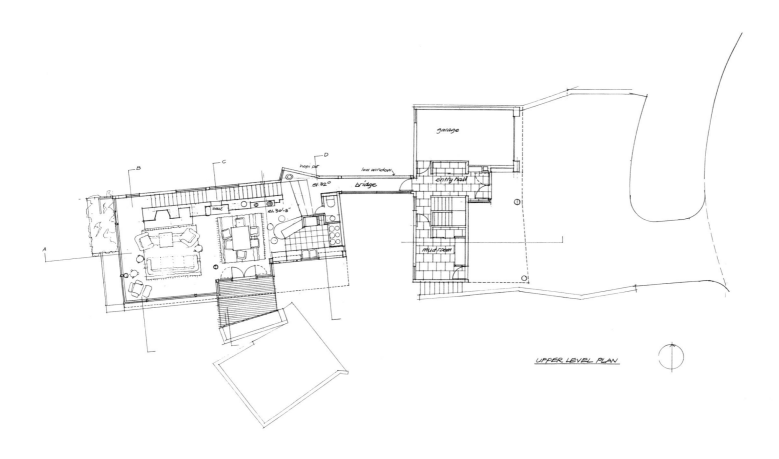

UPPER LEVEL PLAN

*Private residence design drawings. (Courtesy Briner/Strain Architects.)*

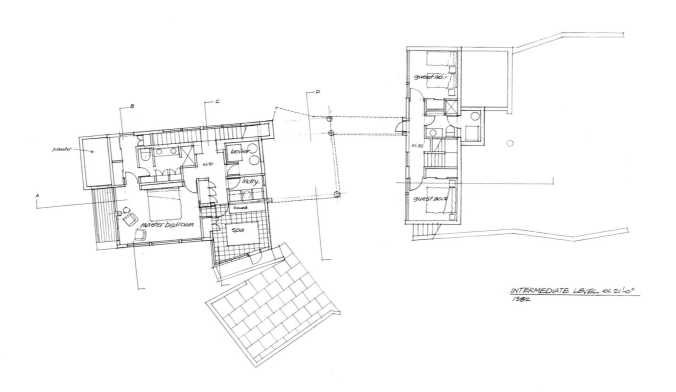

INTERMEDIATE LEVEL el. 21'-0"
1382

*Private residence design drawings. (Courtesy Briner/Strain Architects.)*

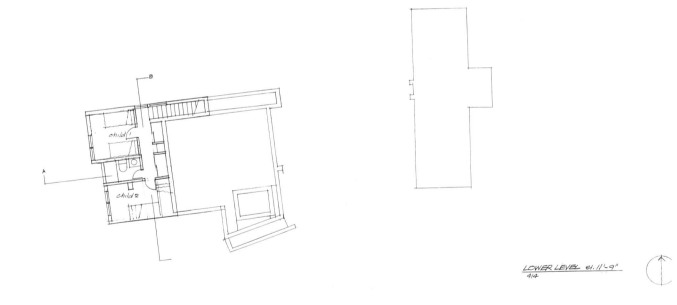

*LOWER LEVEL* el. 11'-9"
4/4

*Private residence design drawings. (Courtesy Briner/Strain Architects.)*

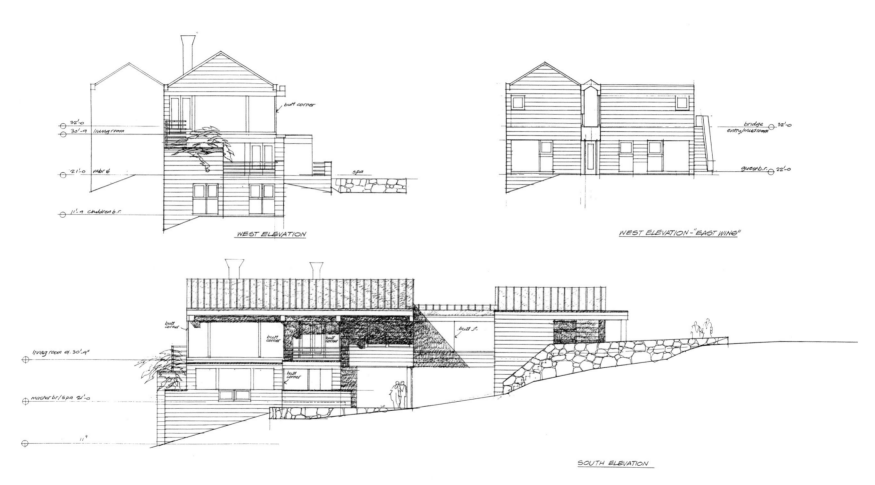

Private residence design drawings. (Courtesy Briner/Strain Architects.)

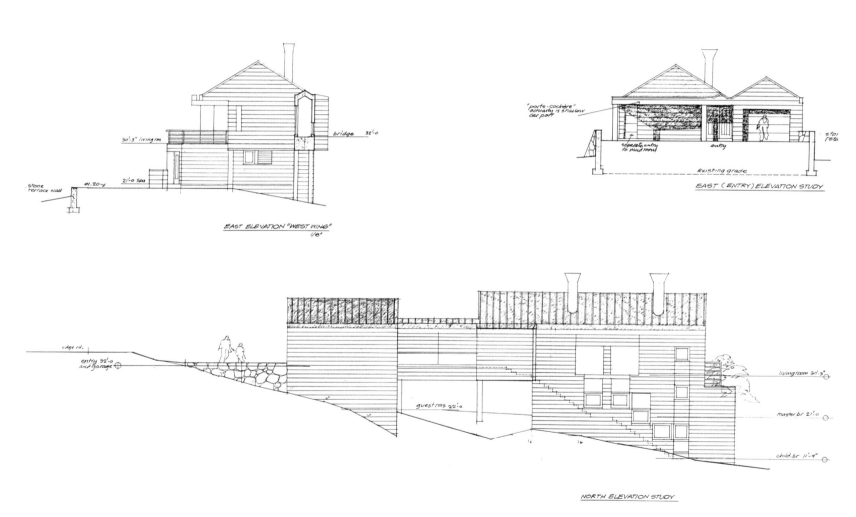

EAST ELEVATION "WEST WING"
1/8"

EAST (ENTRY) ELEVATION STUDY

NORTH ELEVATION STUDY

*Private residence design drawings. (Courtesy Briner/Strain Architects.)*

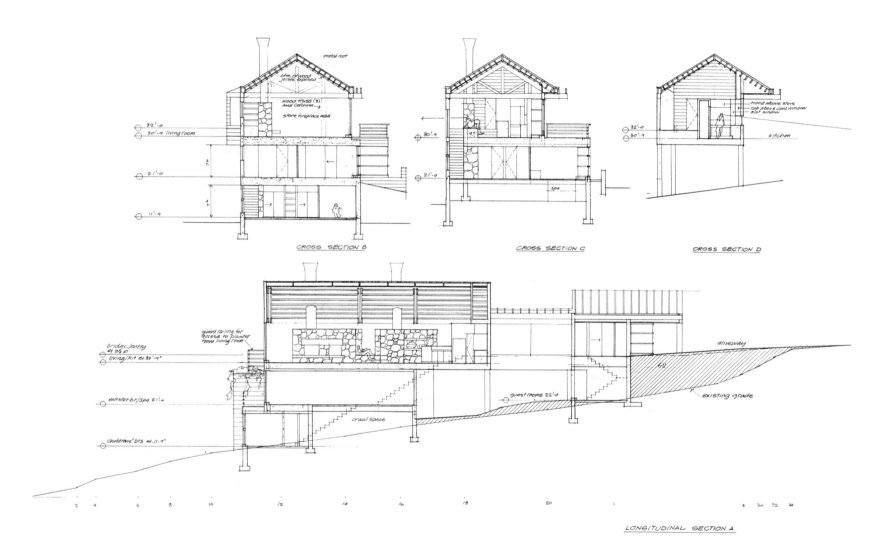

CROSS SECTION B        CROSS SECTION C        CROSS SECTION D

LONGITUDINAL SECTION A

*Private residence design drawings. (Courtesy Briner/Strain Architects.)*

# INDEX

## A

Accessories
    building 74
Acrylic 64
Acrylic model covers 43
Adhesives
    spray-mount 21
    white glue 21
Alignment 71
ASA film speed 104
Assembly of components 71
Atomizer, mouth 14
Automatic exposure mode 104

## B

Background 91, 92
Background paper 94
Balsa 22, 68, 74, 75, 121, 122
Barn doors 96
Base
    color 41
Base topography 33
Basswood 22, 57, 68, 74
Bird's-eye 97
Bracketing exposures 104
Brick masonry 111
Briner, Thomas 128
Brushes
    lettering 13
    paint 14
    watercolor 13
Building accessories 74

## C

Cabinets 80
Camera 93, 102
Camera access 80
Carpet 82
Cars 50
Cedar shakes 117
Ceiling 83
Ceramic tile 78, 120
Chartpac Ad Markers 127
Chipboard 3, 18
Clay 3, 50
Color 127
    edge 69
Color balance 90
Color conversion filter 103
Color slide film 103
Color-balance 103
Colored pencil 25
Complex topography 35
Components 71
Construction sequence 62
Contact vinyl 20, 119
Contours 33
    "slipped sheathing" 37
    smooth, painted 40
    spaced chipboard 39
Contours, topographic 35
Coping saw 12, 37
Cotton 113
Cotton ball 122
Cotton ball trees 48
Cotton balls 118
Covered walks and canopies 74

## D

Depth distortion 105
Design Art Markers, 127
Designer's colors 26
Diffuse sky light 98
Domes 64
Drafting tools 12
Draperies 82

## E

Edge coloring 69
Electric lighting 84
Example building drawings 128
Exposure 104
    bracketing 104
    latitude 104

## F

Fabrics 82
Fabrics, upholstry, carpet 121
Felt-tip markers 23
Field stone masonry 115
Fill light 98
Film 103
Fine-toothed saw 11
Flash 96
Flooring 78
Flooring, wood 119
Fluorescent lamps 96
Foam 18
    expanded polystyrene 18
    extruded polystyrene 18

Foam (continued)
    polyethyene 19
    polystyrene 18
    polyurethane 19
Foam board 4, 61, 121
Foam-sprinkled twigs 47
Focusing 107
Foreground 91
Fountains 53
Furniture 80, 123
    club chair 124
    club sofa 124
    coffee table 126
    dining chair 125
    end table 126
    executive desk 126
    office table 125
    secretarial desk 126
    side chair 124
Furniture layout models 86

**G**

Gable roof 64
Glass 68
Glossy solid colors 118
Gluing 71
Graphite pencil 25
Gravity-formed domes 64
Grid enlargement 32
Grout joints 79

**H**

Hip roof 64
Hobby knife 11
Horizon 93
Hot-wire cutter 4, 15

**I**

Illustration board 55, 61, 68
    Strathmore 17
Incandescent 96
Indian chief 45
Ink 24, 68
Insulating sheathing 39
Interior floors and partitions layout 63
Interior models 77
Interior partitions 79
Interior visibility 59
Intermediate floors 72

**J**

Jig 75

**K**

Knife
    utility 10
    hobby 10

**L**

Laminating plastic 20, 79, 119
Latex-based spackling compound 41
Layout 63
    facade 63
    interior partitions 63
    roof 64
Lens aperture setting 107
Lenses 105
Lettering brushes 13
Lichen 46, 82
Lighting 84
Limestone 114
Logs 79

**M**

Manual grid enlargement 32
Manual mode 104
Markers 23, 78, 114-6, 119, 121, 127
Materials
    chipboard 3
    clay 3
    foam board 4
    polystyrene foam 4
    rendering 66
Medium-scale buildings 59
Midground 92
Model
    construction 9
    cover 43
    design study 1
    design/presentation 1
    furniture designs 123
    furniture layout 86
    interior 77
    photography 88
    photometric 9
    physical size 8
    presentation 1, 5
    site 55
    structural 9
Modeling clay 3
Monofilament fishing line 53
Mortar joints 112
Mouth atomizer 14, 42, 82, 113, 114
Mullions 68

**N**

News releases 88

## O

"On" or "in" the base 60
Opaque projector 30
Outdoor location 90

## P

Paint
  designer's colors 26
  latex 27
  shellac 27
  spray 14
  tempera 25
  watercolor 26
Paintbrushes 14
Paneling 116
Paper trees 48
Pastels 24, 82, 113, 118, 122
Patterned wall covering 122
Pencil
  colored 25
  graphite 25
Periscope-type cameras 102
Perspective control 108
Perspective control (PC) lenses 108
Photo cut-out scale figures 49
Photocopied facades 56
Photocopy enlarging 31
Photoflood 96
Photographic projection 31
Photography
  interior 101
  model 88
Plants 82
Plaster 121
Plaster of paris 54, 58
Plywood 16, 29

Polyethylene foam 19
Polystyrene foam 4, 18
Polyurethane foam 19
Pounce 68
Power tools 15
  hot-wire cutter 15
  sabre saw 15
  table saw 15
Printed plastic trees 47
Prismacolor Art Markers 127
Publicity brochures 88

## Q

Quartz light 96

## R

Railings and balusters 74
Recipes
  brick masonry 111
  ceramic tile 120
  cut limestone 114
  fabric and carpet 121
  field stone 115
  shingles 117
  solid glossy colors 118
  stipple-textured surfaces 113
  wall coverings 122
  wood flooring 119
  wood paneling 116
Reciprocity failure 103
Reflecting pools 52
Reflections 78
Reindeer moss 46, 82
Rendering materials 66
Rock outcroppings 54
Roof 72

Roof layout 64
Roof trusses 83
Roofing shingles 117
Rugs 82
Ruling pen 12, 114, 121, 122

## S

Sabre saw 15
Saw
  coping 12, 37
  sabre 15
Scale 6
Scale figures 49
Scissors 12
Shadows 96
Sheet material selection 61
Shellac 27
Shifting lens 108
Shingles 117
Shrubs 44
  carved foam 47
  reindeer moss 46
Siding 116
Site models 55
Site plan 30
Sky backdrop 91
Sky backdrop lighting 98
Skyline 91, 93
Slide film 103
Slide presentation 89
Slide projector 96
Slide-projected sky 95
Slides 89
Space and depth 91
Spaced chipboard contours 39
Spackling compound 27
Spray paint 14

Spray texture 42
Spray adhesive 21
Stainless steel 80
Stairs 75
Steel wool trees 48
Stipple-textured surfaces 113
Stone 79
Straightedge 11
Strathmore 61
Streams 52
Strobe 96
Stylus 119
Subbase 29
Subbase materials 16
Sunlight 96
Surface rendering 66

## T

Table saw 15
Tapewire 84
Tempera 25, 118, 121, 122
Texture 113
    spray 42
Thistle 46
Tile 120
Tools, hot-wire cutter 4
Toothbrush 113
Topography
    complex 35
    contours 35
    level 33
    simple, nonlevel 33
Trees 44
    cotton ball 48
    foam-sprinkled twigs 47
    Indian Chief 45
    lichen 46

Trees (continued)
    paper 48
    printed plastic 47
    reindeer moss 46
    steel wool 48
    thistle 46
    wire 48
    yarrow 45

## U

Utility knife 10

## V

Vehicles 50
Velour paper 82
View cameras 108
Viewing port 99, 105
Vinyl 20, 78

## W

Water 52
Watercolor 26
Watercolor brushes 13
Waterfalls 53
Weather 90
White glue 21
White-core illustration board 17
Windows and glass 67
Wire trees 48
Wood 57
    balsa 22
    basswood 22
Wood flooring 119
Wood particle board 29
Wood siding and paneling 116
Wood-fiber sheathing board 16

## Y

Yarrow 45

## Z

Zip-a-line 68, 74